W9-CEI-898

Alameda County
LIBRARY
...Infinite possibilities

DONATED
BY
LAM RESEARCH FOUNDATION
AT
COMMUNITY FOUNDATION
SILICON VALLEY

Prehistoric North America

When Land, Sea, and Life Began

The Precambrian

Jean F. Blashfield with Richard P. Jacobs

© 2006 Heinemann Library
a division of Reed Elsevier Inc.
Chicago, Illinois

Customer Service 888-454-2279
Visit our website at www.heinemannlibrary.com

All rights reserved. No part of this publication may be reproduced or transmitted in any form or by any means, electronic or mechanical, including photocopying, recording, taping, or any information storage and retrieval system, without permission in writing from the publisher.

Produced for Heinemann Library by Books Two, Inc.
Editorial: Jean Black, Deborah Grahame
Design: Michelle Lisseter
Illustrations: John T. Wallace, Top-Notch Productions
Picture Research: JLM Visuals
Production: Jean Black

Originated by Modern Age Repro
Printed and bound by South China Printing Company

10 09 08 07 06
10 9 8 7 6 5 4 3 2 1

Library of Congress Cataloging-in-Publication Data

Blashfield, Jean F.
  When land, sea, and life began : the precambrian / Jean F. Blashfield and
Richard P. Jacobs.
      p. cm. -- (Prehistoric North America)
  Includes bibliographical references and index.
  ISBN 1-4034-7657-8
  1. Earth--Juvenile literature. I. Jacobs, Richard P. II. Title. III.
Series: Blashfield, Jean F. Prehistoric North America.
  QB631.4.B575 2005
  560'.171--dc22

                                         2004027391

Geology consultant: Marli Bryant Miller, Ph.D., University of Oregon
Maps: Ronald C, Blakey, Ph.D., Northern Arizona University
PHOTO CREDITS: COVER: Model of Precambrian Jellyfish, Smithsonian National Museum of Natural History; Stromatolites in the Bahamas, NOAA/NURP. TITLE PAGE: Rift through Iceland, Breck P. Kent
INTERIOR: The Alfred Wegener Institute for Polar and Marine Research: 24; Atkins, Kyle: 47; Balkwell, David: 72 Archean; Crangle, Charlie: 73 Jurassic; The Field Museum: 8, 72 Cambrian, Silurian, Permian, 73 Paleocene, Miocene, Pliocene; Gilbert, Gordon R: 30 left, 73 Eocene; Jacobs, Richard P.: 5, 11, 13, 14, 17 left, 17 right, 18, 19 right, 19 top, 19 bot, 38, 39 top, 40, 41, 42, 46, 48 top, 51, 55 center, 55 top left, 55 top right, 57 bot, 66 bot, 70; Kent, Breck P.: 6, 9, 22, 25, 43 top, 43 bot, 55 bot left, 55 bot right, 58 top, 72 Ordovician, Devonian, Mississippian, 73 Holocene; Larson, Alden: 10; Laudon, Lowell R.: 69; Leszczynski, Zig: 73 Oligocene; Miller, Marli: Page borders, 39 bot, 50, 61, 64, 68 left, 68 right, 73 Pleistocene; NASA: 4, 35, 58 bot, 72 Hadean; NOAA: 27, 32, 66 top; Nicol, Keith: 36; Smithsonian Nat'l Museum of Natural History: 67, 71, 72 Proterozoic, Pennsylvanian; Snead, Rodman E.: 30 right, 43 center, 59; University of Michigan Exhibit Museum: 73 Triassic; USGS: 7, 33, 48 bot; Young, Simon R.: 44; Zitzer, Marypat: 52, 54 top, 54 bot, 57 top.

Every effort has been made to contact copyright holders of any material reproduced in this book. Any omissions will be rectified in subsequent printings if notice is given to the publisher.

Some words are shown in bold, **like this**. You can find the definitions for these words in the glossary.

Contents

Chapter 1

The First Days of Earth

Our Earth formed about 4.6 billion years ago. There was no North America then. There were no continents, or even oceans. There was just a collection of stuck-together dust particles and rocks. It circled a star—our sun—with other similar spheres.

The new planet was not even hot at first. But gradually so much material was added on that pressure began to heat the material deep inside. The heat melted the solid material enough for heavy chemical elements, such as iron, to sink through the fluid material into the center. The planet's **core** eventually developed. It was rich in iron and other heavy metals.

↳ *Iron meteorites from outer space such as this one contributed to building the core of Earth.*

The first billion years of the planet's existence were years of almost constant pounding by **meteorites**. These rocks from the solar system crashed into the surface. They sank into the hot interior and melted. The materials of which the meteorites were made became part of the planet. They provided many elements that are important in our lives today.

Any atmosphere that existed was turned to vapor by the impacts and was blasted away. Eventually, though, an atmosphere formed faster from gases within the planet than could be vaporized. This young atmosphere prevented more meteorites from crashing to the surface. They were usually burned up by friction from the new air before they could reach the surface.

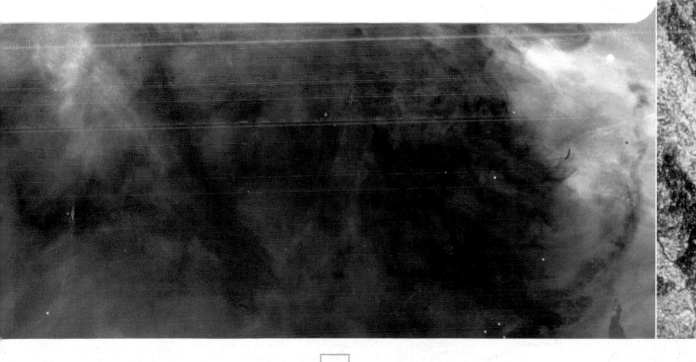

The atmosphere was not one that we could breathe. It was a thick stew of poisonous gases, such as methane and ammonia. These gases bubbled up from inside the hot planet. Earth's atmosphere then may have resembled the atmospheres of Jupiter and Saturn today.

At first, the surface of the planet was hot enough to remain melted, or **molten**. But some molten material with less **density** rose to the surface, cooled, and then hardened into rock. The rock floated on the denser molten material beneath it.

↶ *Fog, mist, rain, and ocean all came from the water vapor that was in the early atmosphere.*

The new rock jostled and swayed, colliding with other rock. Sometimes the two kinds of rock remained attached. They accumulated into larger masses of rock. These masses became permanent enough to be called the planet's **crust**. The first crust that has been dated did not form until the planet had already existed for at least 600 million years.

There was no water on the early planet because the surface was too hot. However, there was some water vapor in the new atmosphere. As the planet gradually cooled, water vapor turned to rain. Over millions of more years, that rain cooled the surface. Water flowed and became rivers and ocean.

Iron had sunk to the core of the planet, but the layer above it, called the **mantle**, remained very hot. The mantle makes up 80 percent of the entire bulk of the planet. It is mostly solid rock, but some of the rock near the crust becomes molten, or melts. Molten material of the mantle is called **magma**.

When magma reaches the surface of the planet, such as in a volcano, it is called **lava**. Magma and the crystals it contains make up the source of all the rock, islands, seafloor, and continents on our planet.

Lava pouring from a volcano may have come from the mantle.

Earth's Calendar

Most people had long believed that Earth had existed for only a few thousand years. Then, in the late 18th century, they began to accept a new theory. This theory proposed that Earth's history involved time periods much longer than anyone had ever imagined before. Naturalists developed a new kind of calendar. It is based primarily on the presence of **fossils**, the remains of living things, in rocks. Their calendar is the **geologic time scale**.

Naturalists divided time into different periods. They based these divisions of time on the fossil evidence they found in layers of rock. Geologists (and **paleontologists**, the scientists who study fossils) started their new geologic time scale at the time from which they found many fossils of animals with hard shells.

A museum artist's idea of what Earth might have looked like before life began

The scientists thought that hard-shelled living things were probably the first living things. They called the period from which these animals came the Cambrian. This name is based on the old name for Wales, where important discoveries were made. All Earth history before living things was called *Pre*cambrian.

Almost a hundred years later, however, paleontologists discovered many living things that had lived before Cambrian times. By then, the name *Precambrian* had been firmly cast in stone and is still used.

Precambrian time was much longer than the time starting with the Cambrian. The Precambrian includes 88 percent of Earth's history. That is from about 4.6 billion years ago to about 543 million years ago. Geologists now call the time period that has occurred since 543 million years ago the Phanerozoic **Eon**, meaning "revealed life."

Geologists now divide Precambrian time into three major time periods. The Hadean Eon is approximately the first 600 million years. There is almost no record in rocks of what was happening. The name *Hadean* comes from "Hades," which is the classical Greek name for the Underworld or Hell. (This period is also called Pre-Archean.)

The Archean Eon (also written *Archaean*, which comes from the Greek for "ancient" or "beginning") is the next 1.3 billion years. It started at 3.96 billion years ago, which is the date given for the earliest known rocks. (Note that these early times are all approximations.)

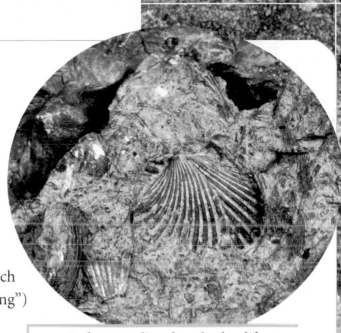

↺ *Early naturalists thought that life started with shelled animals like the brachiopods that made these fossils.*

	Time Period	Tectonic Events	Biological Events	
PRECAMBRIAN TIME • 4.5 billion to 543 million years ago	**Hadean Eon** *4.5–3.96 billion years ago* Named for Hades, or Hell	No Earth rocks from this time found	None	
	Archean Eon *3.96–2.5 billion years ago* ame means "Ancient"	Oldest known rocks First permanent crust First stable continents	Seawater formed First bacteria Atmosphere formed	
	Proterozoic Eon *2.5 billion–543 million*	North American craton formed First iron–bearing sediments First large glaciation Formation and breakup of Rodinia supercontinent Gondwana, southern supercontinent, formed	Free oxygen in atmosphere First nucleated cells, allowing sexual reproduction First multicellular animals First animals with exoskeletons First fungi	

PALEOZOIC ERA • *543 to 248 million years ago*
MESOZOIC ERA • *248 to 65 million years ago*
CENOZOIC ERA • *65 million years ago to present*

The photo on the outside edges of each of the pages in this book is of Archean **quartzite** rock that was found by geologists in Wyoming.

The last major span of time in the Precambrian is the Proterozoic Eon. In Greek, the term *Proterozoic* means "former life." It lasted from 2.5 billion years to 543 million years ago. It is usually divided into three parts—Early, Middle, and Late Proterozoic. As we'll see in later chapters, important events, both in the geologic development of Earth and in its living things, occurred during the Proterozoic Eon.

Measuring Time

The naturalists studying fossils and rocks figured out the general order in which various plants or animals appeared. If a rock contained fossils of animal A, and it was underneath another rock containing fossils of animal B, the naturalists could infer that animal A was older than animal B.

This kind of dating does not give specific ages, only order. Called **relative dating**, it is useful primarily in **sedimentary rocks**. Sedimentary rocks are rocks that formed as hardened layers of **sediment** in oceans, lakes, rivers, and even deserts.

↰ *Geologists exploring a cliff face with layers of sedimentary rock that might contain fossils*

The fossil of a Precambrian jellyfish ↱
found in sedimentary rock

Sedimentary layers can be turned upside down, perhaps by an earthquake. The evidence of fossils found in the rock will show in what order the layers were originally formed.

Until the 1940s, relative dating was the only way to date rocks. At that time, a process called radiometric dating was invented. Radiometric dating indicates **absolute time**. It is based on the knowledge that certain radioactive elements change, or decay, at a known, predictable rate. Scientists can determine the ages of many different rocks by measuring the amount of **radioactive decay** that has taken place.

*The **folding** of rock layers ↱*
can change the order in
which fossils are found.

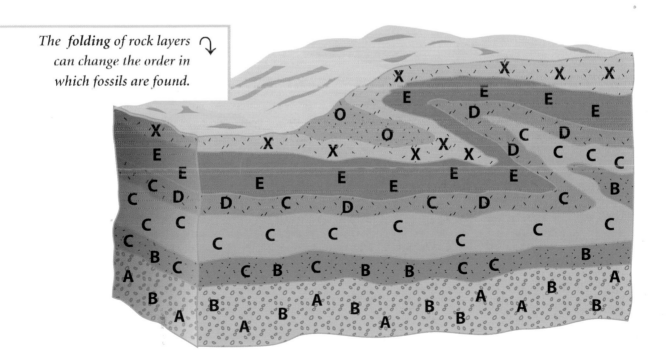

HOW DO THEY KNOW
The Ages of Rocks?

PARTICLES GIVEN OFF

PROTON

NEUTRON

RADIATION EMITTED

The nucleus, or center, of some atoms is unstable. It gives off particles until there are no extra particles left to give off. At that time, the atoms have become a different element. This change, or decay, happens at a known, predictable rate. This rate is called the element's half-life. The half-life is the time it takes for one-half of the atoms in a sample to turn into another element.

In the diagram of radioactive decay at the left, different kinds of particles are being given off by the radioactive nucleus of an atom. Some atoms give off enough particles that, over time, the nucleus loses a whole proton or neutron. If it loses a neutron, it becomes a different form of the same element. But if it loses a proton, it becomes a different chemical element.

Geologists can measure the elements in a rock and calculate how long they have been undergoing change. This kind of dating is used most often with igneous rocks. Uranium, carbon, and potassium are among the elements used in determining the absolute ages, or ages in years, of rocks and other materials. Geologists working in the field can identify radioactive rock by using an instrument called a Geiger counter that beeps when it measures particles being given off by the chemical elements in the rock.

One of the most useful minerals for dating rocks is zircon. This mineral is very resistant to change. It generally remains the same, even under extreme heat, pressure, and erosion. However, zircon contains a form of the element uranium, which undergoes radioactive decay. Some of the oldest minerals found and dated by radiometric methods have been zircons.

Zircons found in the Beartooth Mountains of Wyoming and Montana have been dated to almost 4 billion years. Geologists were able to date them despite the fact that the **metamorphic rock** around them dates to only 2.8 billion years. These ages tell us that the original rock of the Beartooth Mountains formed about 4 billion years ago.

The mineral zircon is found in many different colors. The radioactive uranium in zircon's chemical formula can be used for dating rocks.

Earth's Distant Future

Over the eons, the great heat of the mantle came mostly from radioactive elements. These elements gave off heat when high-energy particles escaped from the nuclei of the atoms. Scientists think that in its early days Earth may have had a temperature of 18,000°F (10,000°C). The heat gradually cooled as these elements changed into stable form. Today, the core's temperature is about half that. Someday, far, far in the future, the planet may cool enough for all activity to stop. Earth will be a dead planet.

Chapter 2

The Structure of the Planet

At the center of Earth is the core. It consists of two layers. The innermost part is a solid sphere, about the size of our moon. It is probably made of an alloy, or mixture, of iron and perhaps nickel, with some other elements mixed in. It has a density of about 10.7 grams per cubic centimeter. This solid portion is about 1,516 miles (2,440 km) in diameter. Surrounding the solid core is a liquid core of the same metals.

The liquid part of the core plays an important role in giving the planet a **magnetic field**. A magnetic field is formed whenever electrons (the negative particles in an atom) move. The movement of **electrons** is electricity. Earth itself has a magnetic field. That field is what makes a compass work in helping a person find north. The magnetized needle in a compass aligns itself with Earth's magnetic field.

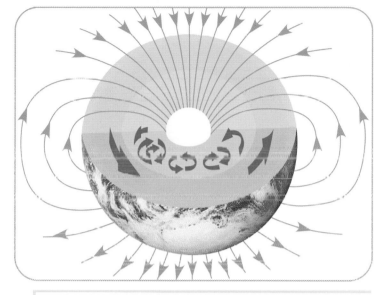

Earth's magnetic field is stronger at the poles than at the equator. It is formed by the movement of liquid iron in the core.

The material in the fluid core moves in a complex pattern. The pattern results both from heat and the spin of the planet. The movement creates a magnetic field for the planet that extends out into space. The pull of the magnetic field is very strong at the poles. It grows weaker the closer one goes to the equator.

At some places on Earth's crust, such as at Yellowstone National Park, heat from the planet's interior turns water into steam.

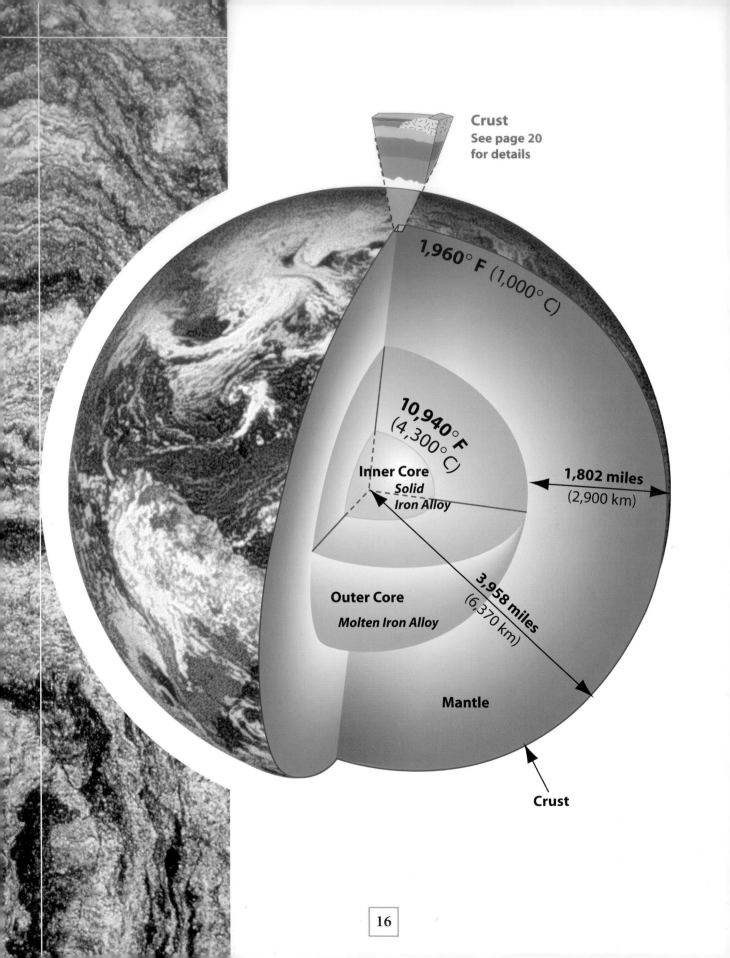

Crust
See page 20
for details

1,960° F (1,000° C)

10,940° F
(4,300° C)

Inner Core
*Solid
Iron Alloy*

1,802 miles
(2,900 km)

3,958 miles
(6,370 km)

Outer Core
Molten Iron Alloy

Mantle

Crust

Above the core is the mantle. Instead of being metallic like the core, it is primarily made up of various nonmetallic minerals in solid rock. Minerals are natural, nonliving solids. The atoms in minerals are arranged in an orderly pattern called crystalline. A crystal of table salt, for example, is an orderly pattern of the atoms of sodium and chlorine.

↰ *Silicates, which are compounds containing silicon and oxygen, are the most abundant minerals. This silicate is mica.*

Olivine is the main mineral making up Earth's mantle. It is a silicate rich in iron or magnesium. ↱

The mantle is the largest part of the planet. It is about 1,802 miles (2,900 km) thick. The main elements in the mantle are oxygen, silicon, iron, and magnesium. They often combine to form the minerals that are the main ingredients in igneous rocks. All other elements exist in varying amounts. The material in the mantle is less than half as dense as the material that makes up the core.

Many rocks form within the mantle when different minerals mix and then harden. Sometimes, though, chunks of rock form that are different from the rock in which they are found. These rocks may then reach the surface as part of volcanic eruptions. Such odd rocks are called **xenoliths**, meaning "foreign rocks." Geologists hunt for xenoliths, hoping to learn more about the materials that make up the mantle.

Earth's Crust

Much of the upper portion of the mantle is called the **asthenosphere**, for the Greek word meaning "weak." More mantle lies above the asthenosphere. This mantle is solid and is attached to the crust, on which we live. This solid upper mantle and the crust are, together, called the **lithosphere**. This term comes from the Greek word *litho*, meaning "rock."

Inspecting a Xenolith

As Highway I winds around the many lakes of Western Ontario, Canada, **outcrops**, or exposed portions, of rock are endlessly in view. These outcrops expose varieties of crystalline, Precambrian rock. Upon closer inspection, xenoliths can be seen in some of the exposed rock. Fragments of dark-colored rock show clearly against the lighter-colored **granite**. Granite is one of the most common igneous rocks.

Molten granite probably invaded spaces in a darker-colored mass of pre-existing rock. Fragments of that dark rock broke loose. They became included in the magma that is derived from granite. The crystals of the granite are large. This shows that its magma must have cooled slowly. Such slow cooling indicates that the magma was deep beneath the surface as it cooled and incorporated the dark xenoliths.

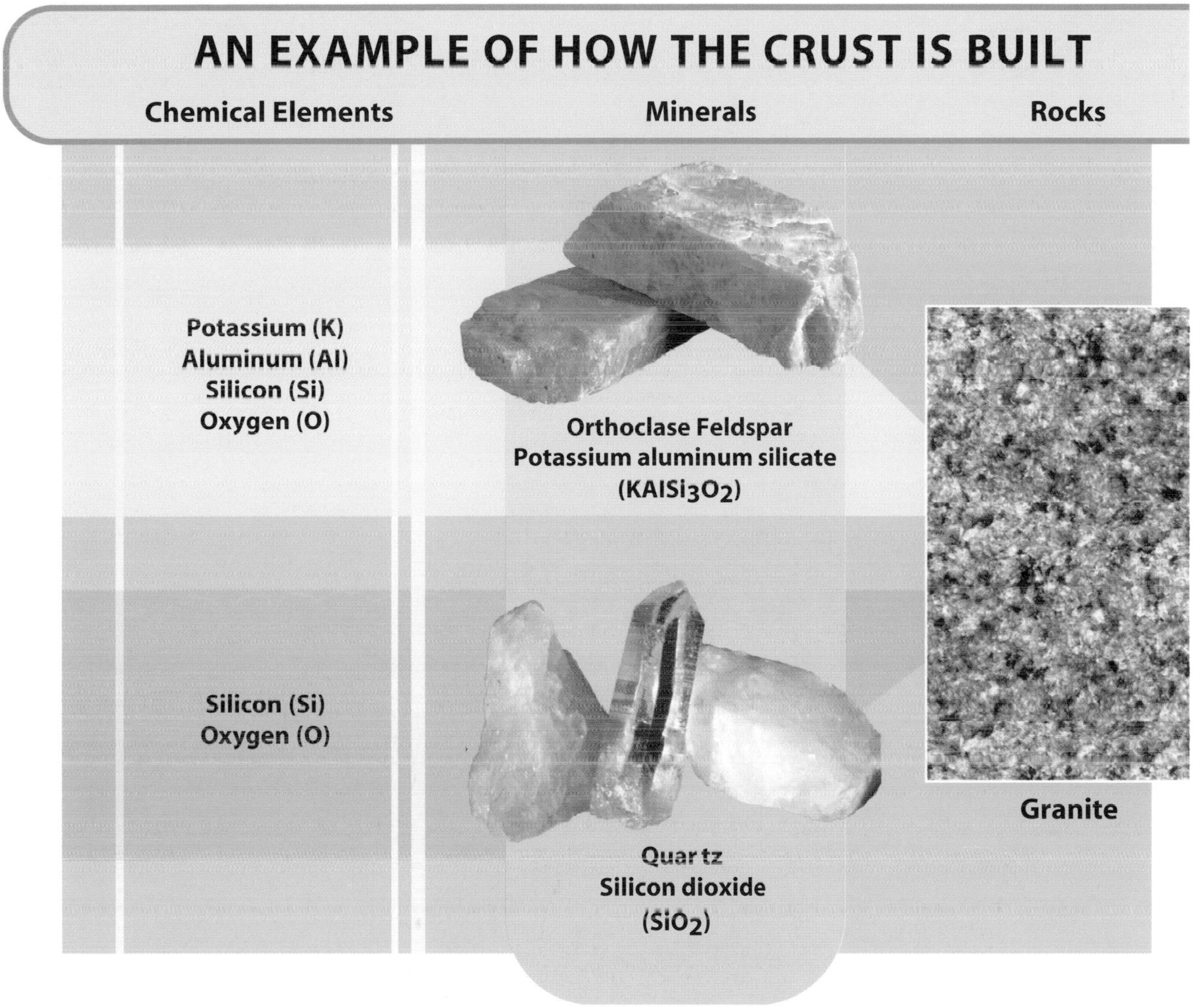

AN EXAMPLE OF HOW THE CRUST IS BUILT

Chemical Elements	Minerals	Rocks

Potassium (K)
Aluminum (Al)
Silicon (Si)
Oxygen (O)

Orthoclase Feldspar
Potassium aluminum silicate
$(KAlSi_3O_2)$

Granite

Silicon (Si)
Oxygen (O)

Quartz
Silicon dioxide
(SiO_2)

The crust and the mantle are separated by a sudden change in character. This break is called the Mohorovicic discontinuity, often referred to as the Moho. This difference in character, or discontinuity, was named for a Croatian geologist, Andrija Mohorovicic (1857-1936), who first suggested that there must be such a break.

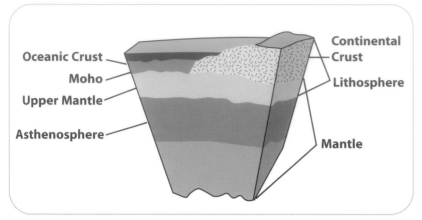

Oceanic Crust
Moho
Upper Mantle
Asthenosphere

Continental Crust
Lithosphere
Mantle

The rocks above and below the Moho are quite different. Rock above the Moho is strong, but it tends to break under pressure. It is also less dense than the rock below the Moho. The rock below tends to flow. It's still solid, but it changes shape under pressure.

The earth's crust consists of two different kinds of material—oceanic crust and continental crust. The oceans are not just water that has accumulated in low spots in Earth's crust. Instead, the crust beneath the oceans is quite different in density and character from the crust making up the continents.

Oceanic crust is about 3 to 7 miles (5 to 12 km) thick and has an average density of 3.0 grams per cubic centimeter. It is rich in the elements magnesium and iron. Oceanic crust tends to be lower in elevation than continental crust. This is because it is made of thinner, denser material.

Continental crust is an average of about 22 miles (35 km) thick and is less dense, about 2.7 grams per cubic centimeter. It is richer in the mineral called **silica**.

Discovering the Inside of the Planet

Seismic waves are waves of energy that spread out from a disturbance in the rock of Earth's crust. The word *seismic* comes from the Greek word for "earthquake." Disturbance of the crust can occur during an earthquake or any rock movement. The energy waves can be detected and recorded on instruments called seismomenters. Because earthquakes send out seismic energy waves in all directions, scientists all over the world know when an earthquake happens.

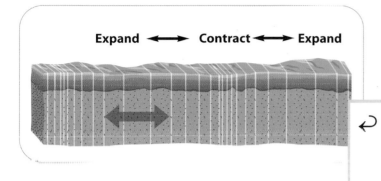

Expand ←→ Contract ←→ Expand

P waves expand and contract the material as they move through both rock and liquid. These changes happen in the direction the wave is moving.

Energy waves that travel through the Earth change direction when the material they are moving through changes. They change speed when the temperature changes. The waves are of two types. Primary waves, called P-waves, alternately compress and expand the particles in rock. They compress and expand in the same direction as the energy wave is moving as it passes through. P-waves are the faster of the two types. They can travel through both solid rock and liquid.

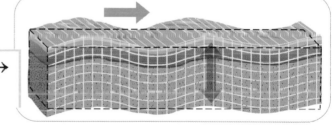

S waves are slower and they move material at right angles to the direction of the wave.

Secondary waves, or S-waves, are vibrations that occur at right angles to the direction of the wave. S-waves travel only through solid rock. They bounce off liquid deep within the planet and change the direction they are moving.

Seismometers are located in laboratories and remote areas all over Earth. Scientists know immediately when something has jarred the rock of the planet. They know how different kinds of liquid and solid rocks change the movement of the two types of waves. This information lets them determine the makeup of the earth by studying how those waves behave as they travel through Earth's different layers.

Chapter 3

An Absurd Idea

Our world maps today, and those of three hundred years ago, show North America in the same place. But this continent hasn't always been where it is now. Throughout most of Earth's history, the continents have drifted. They still are drifting today. But the movement is so slow that your children and your children's grandchildren won't notice any difference.

Our knowledge of the movement of the continents—originally called **continental drift**—is quite new. Since the 1960s, two ideas have become basic to our knowledge of Earth's structure. The first idea is that the entire lithosphere of the earth—both continents and oceans—is broken up into a series of plates. Twelve plates are quite large and several are small. The small ones fit in between the nooks and crannies of the big ones. Most of North America, along with much of the Atlantic Ocean and some of Asia, is on one plate called the North American plate. The second idea is that these plates move and probably always have been moving. This movement has been called "the dance of the continents."

The study of the crust, its structure, and movement is called **plate tectonics**. *Tectonics* is a Greek word meaning "to build." So "plate tectonics" is the science of how Earth's surface is built of **tectonic plates**, how these plates are formed, how they can be destroyed, and how they interact with each other.

Geologists are interested in plate tectonics because of what happens where the plates meet. Earthquakes, volcanoes, and mountain building are events that result from plate tectonics. They all happen in response to the movement of tectonic plates and their interactions at the boundaries between them.

The man who is now called the "Father of Continental Drift" was a German scientist named Alfred Wegener. He studied changes in the planet's climates that had taken place since ancient times. In his studies, Wegener became convinced that the continents had moved since ancient times. He also believed that they were continuing to move today, and that they had once been joined in a single big continent, or **supercontinent**.

Most geologists found Wegener's idea absurd and refused to consider it. It took the work of many scientists over many years to demonstrate that Wegener had been right all along.

Alfred Wegener, The Father of Continental Drift

Alfred Lothar Wegener was born in Berlin, Germany, in 1880. He studied meteorology (weather and climate) and became a professor at Marburg University. He was most interested in the way climates have changed during the past. He and other scientists studied ancient climates by analyzing fossil remains. They compared the remains to the living things of today and the kinds of climates they require for life.

Though others laughed at Wegener for his idea of continental drift, he clung to the idea. He had plenty of evidence that continents had moved, but he could not explain just how they moved. He wrote up his ideas in *The Origin of Continents and Oceans*, published first in 1915, and revised three times before his death. In 1930, he was still trying to prove his ideas while working at a weather station on the ice cap of Greenland. As winter closed in, he failed to leave the station on time to reach safety, and he froze to death. He didn't know that years later his

Matching Continents Across Oceans

Some scientists in the 19th century had already provided information that Wegener used in his work. They had puzzled over the fact that various fossils had been found in one kind of climate even though the fossils must have originated in a different climate.

Fossils of a tropical plant called *Glossopteris*, for example, had been found in the far north. *Glossopteris* was a primitive, tree-like fern. This fossil had also been found in both southern Africa and southern South America. This plant and its relatives were the main type of vegetation in tropical regions 270 million years ago.

A few of the scientists who found fossils in odd places came up with an idea. They wondered if very long land bridges had once connected the continents.

↩ *A fossil of a* Glossopteris *seed fern leaf*

↪ *Naturalists used today's location of fossils of* Glossopteris *(left) as evidence that these locations had once been joined in a supercontinent (right).*

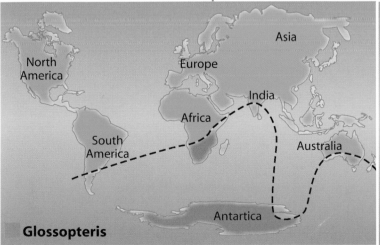
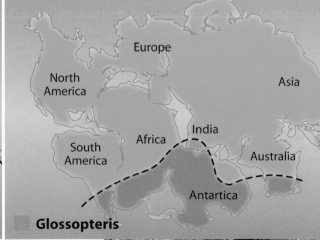

Austrian geologist Eduard Suess also traced identical rock formations. They were identical, yet located on opposite shores of two continents. He proposed that South America, Africa, India, Australia, and Antarctica had all once been a southern supercontinent. But he assumed that parts of this supercontinent had sunk to become oceans. He gave no thought to the possibility that the continents had broken apart and actually moved.

Wegener studied all he could find on the subject of rock formations and fossils matching each other across oceans. He located the remains of huge **reef** systems (like coral reefs today) that matched each other on opposite sides of the Atlantic Ocean. He also found deposits of material moved by ancient **glaciers** that matched up in the same way.

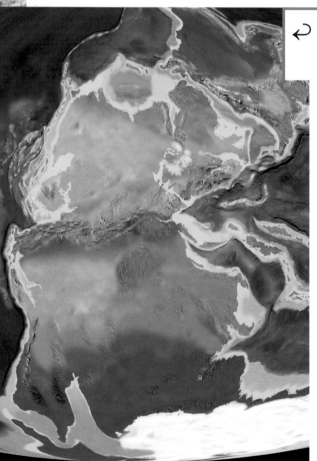

Wegener proposed the idea that a supercontinent he called Pangea once existed. He could not have made this map of Pangea, however, because he did not have enough evidence.

Wegener made a startling proposal—suppose ALL the continents were once attached to each other in one huge supercontinent? Various things he knew about ancient climates would then be explained. He called his supercontinent Pangea (sometimes written *Pangaea*), which comes from the Greek words meaning "all earth."

Because Wegener couldn't explain how the supercontinent could have split apart, let alone moved, few other scientists took him seriously. After all, they were certain that the continents are deeply rooted in the earth and that they are very stable—they couldn't have moved! During the 1950s and 1960s, however, other evidence came along that fit nicely into the puzzle Wegener had proposed.

Evidence in the Ocean

During the 1950s, the U.S. Navy decided that its submarine program needed accurate maps of the seafloor. Oceanographers and geologists had long known that there is a long high ridge of underwater mountains. This ridge runs from north to south through the middle of the Atlantic Ocean. Called the Mid-Atlantic Ridge, it consists of mountains formed by lava rising upward from the mantle. Lava comes up through a long, wide valley opening in the ridge. As the lava rises, the two sides of this valley are pushed farther and farther apart. This process is called **seafloor spreading**.

The Mid-Atlantic Ridge is about 1,250 miles (2,000 km) wide and rises more than 1 mile (2 km)

Vents through which very hot water escapes are located along the ocean ridges. ↻

above the seafloor. The Navy found that similar mountain ranges are located in a line that twists and turns through all Earth's oceans, like the stitches on a baseball. These **ocean ridges** make up a mountain chain about 50,000 miles (80,000 km) long.

Geologists measured the ages of rocks in the seafloor. They found that rock near an ocean ridge is younger than the rock farther from the ridge. This means that new seafloor was built up at the ridge. It then was gradually pushed toward the continents by even more new seafloor. Geologists realized an astonishing fact. Although continental rock can be several billion years old, nowhere in the ocean is the seafloor more than about 200 million years old!

But where did the older seafloor go? Hugo Benioff, an American seismologist, found that earthquakes occur in huge numbers along a deep **trench** in the floor of the Pacific Ocean. It seemed to him that a lot of rock was moving and breaking in that trench.

He proposed that perhaps the ocean floor destroys itself at trenches by moving downward into the mantle. Earthquakes occur when parts of the descending ocean floor suddenly slip downward.

Geologists also began to explore the idea that Earth's magnetic field has reversed itself at various times in the planet's history. A north-seeking compass would suddenly seek south instead. Scientists all over the world found that magnetic flip-flops had taken place everywhere on the planet at the same times. It has been 780,000 years since it flipped the last time.

Why was this important? When igneous rock hardens, any iron-containing minerals within it record the magnetic field of Earth at the location where it was formed. As we saw in the diagram on page 15, the magnetic field is stronger near the poles than near the equator.

A sample of rock can be taken to the laboratory to have the magnetic field measured. Geologists can tell if the rock was moved from where it was formed. They can also tell if Earth's magnetic field changed after the rock was formed. Geologists found that magnestism in seafloor rocks recorded their original location on the seafloor where they hardened.

↶ *The red lines on this globe of Earth show ocean ridges. The yellow lines show where seafloor disappears.*

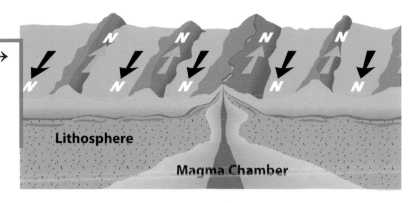

Earth's magnetic field flipped from north (N) and back again. These changes were recorded in newly hardened rock as it moved away from an ocean ridge.

Lithosphere

Magma Chamber

The evidence for continental drift was mounting up. However, geologists still needed an explanation for how individual continents could drift. In 1965, a Canadian physicist-turned-geologist, J. Tuzo Wilson, published a short paper. The paper pulled together all the information on the subject.

Wilson described the evidence and reached the conclusion that the planet's crust must ride on rigid plates of lithosphere, and that these plates drifted. He stated that important Earth-events happen at the boundaries of those plates.

The Making of Seafloor

There was plenty of evidence that seafloor spreading creates new crust. This new crust pushes plates apart, or makes them diverge. **Divergent** boundaries occur at ocean ridges.

The ocean ridge system is the largest single physical feature on the planet. This system is almost never seen, however. It is as though a land feature as spectacular as the Himalayas were hidden beneath the deepest sea, where no one could climb or even admire them.

The mountains built up at the Mid-Atlantic Ridge may be 13,000 feet (4,000 km) high. Even so, their crests rarely come within 6,500 feet (2,000 m) of sea level. The exception is the island of Iceland in the North Atlantic. The island is actually part of the Mid-Atlantic Ridge.

Part of Iceland lies on the North American plate and part lies on the Eurasian plate. The two plate edges currently come within 33 feet (10 m) of each other through the middle of the island. The photo on the title page of this book shows the gap between the two plates.

Walking Between Europe
and North America

Iceland is the only place where the Mid-Atlantic Ridge rises out of the sea. The island was formed by outpourings of **basalt** lava that built up until it was above sea level. The edges of the North American plate and the Eurasian plate are visible. They are moving apart, but this movement is too slow to be noticed by the human eye.

A **rift**, or separation, is located where the Mid-Atlantic Ridge runs through the island. A person walking along the rift sees the same type of geologic activity that takes place unseen beneath the surface of the Atlantic Ocean. There is evidence of spreading—the area is covered with new volcanic rock, and lines of fracture are seen along the rift. Frequent volcanic eruptions on Iceland cause the island to continue to grow by the addition of lava.

The presence of hot springs and **geysers** in Iceland indicate how close to the surface the heat of the mantle comes. Many Icelanders use the natural heat of their island to heat their homes and water.

The new crust that forms at ocean ridges is made of the igneous rock called basalt. It is estimated that 1.5 inches (40 mm) of new crust is added to each side of an ocean ridge each year. Growth doesn't necessarily happen evenly, however. Some parts of the ridge grow faster than other parts. This difference causes **faults**, or breaks, to occur at right angles to the ocean ridge. Called **transform faults**, these breaks are often the site of shallow earthquakes.

There are many transform faults along the 50,000-mile (80,000-km) length of the ocean ridge system. The breaking of rock at these faults account for the fact that geological instruments record more than a million earthquakes a year. Fortunately, humans rarely feel them.

Recycled Seafloor

But if new seafloor is always being created, why doesn't Earth get bigger and bigger?

Geologists came to accept Benioff's idea that old seafloor disappears back into the mantle. The long, narrow trenches where old seafloor goes are called **subduction** zones. Oceanic crust material may be subducted (meaning "led under") into a trench. The trench eventually takes it back deep into the mantle where the rock is recycled.

Trenches occur where two plates move toward each other, or converge. They form a **convergent** boundary. If the margins, or edges, of both plates consist of continental crust, the two masses of land are of the same density. They smash into each other, and the colliding land rises, forming mountains. If an oceanic plate meets a continental plate, the more dense oceanic crust is forced under the less dense continental crust. The downward movement of the oceanic crust creates a trench.

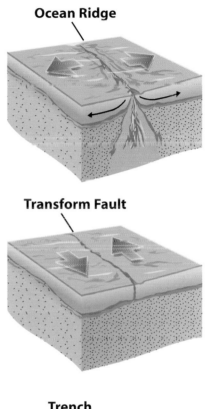

Ocean Ridge

Transform Fault

Trench

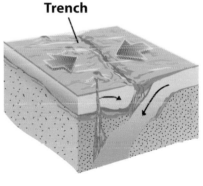

↻ *Seafloor is formed at an ocean ridge (top). As it moves away, it may break at a transform fault (center). Finally, it disappears down a trench (bottom). Volcanoes form as a result.*

Oceanographers have found twenty trenches in the ocean. These trenches total about 13,670 miles (22,000 km). The largest ones lie parallel to continental mountain ranges, such as the Andes in South America. The deepest trench is the Marianas Trench in the western Pacific.

Continental Margins

The presence of a trench near the edge, or margin, of a continent determines what kind of geologic activity occurs there. When there is no trench, the margin is inactive. That doesn't mean nothing at all happens.

Sediment, such as sand eroded from mountains, collects at an inactive, or quiet, margin. Carried by rivers, it collects on the **continental shelf**, that portion of a continent that extends into the ocean. This shelf drops down gently near the shore. Farther out, it drops more abruptly, in what is called the continental slope.

Into the Deepest Trench

In 1960, Jacques Piccard and Navy lieutenant Don Walsh used a specially built submersible craft to descend into the Challenger Deep, the deepest portion of the Marianas Trench. Their vehicle, named the *Trieste*, did not have its own power. Instead, it had to be dropped into the trench and then hauled back up on a huge pulley. The two men descended for a period of over four hours to a depth of 35,810 feet (10,915 m). During the minutes they were at the bottom of the trench there was 7 miles (11.3 km) of ocean above them. Radio and TV listeners the world over breathed a sigh of relief when the craft emerged from the sea. Piccard and Walsh's deep-diving record has never been broken.

On North America's eastern coast, the shelf may extend nearly 300 miles (500 km) before dropping into the much steeper continental slope. Sediment that builds up on continental shelves hardens into sedimentary rock.

North America's west coast is the continent's active plate boundary. The continental shelf is rarely more than a mile or two wide. The steeper continental slope drops into a trench where subduction occurs. The most famous part of California's active margin is the San Andreas Fault.

When an oceanic plate is subducting below a continental plate, shallow earthquakes occur. This happens as the two plates stick together briefly and then jerk apart. Then, as the plate moves deeper into the mantle and begins to break apart, earthquakes located deep within the planet occur.

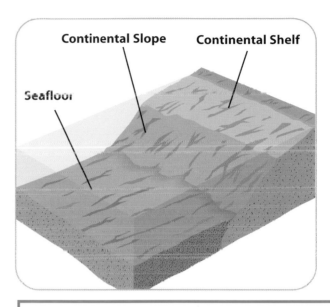

 The continental shelf forms the shallow sea where sediment built up and where life began.

It is not only earthquakes that occur as oceanic plate material moves down into the mantle. Volcanoes also occur. The heated water contained in the plate material is drawn into the lithosphere above it. The heat melts some of the lithosphere. This material may rise to the surface as fresh lava spewing out of volcanoes.

Volcanoes may form inland from a trench when lava from the melting lithosphere rises through the land.

What Moves the Plates?

After the idea of plate tectonics was accepted, geologists assumed that the plates moved because of circular currents called convection cells in the mantle beneath them. **Convection currents** are the same currents that gradually heat all the liquid in a pot on a stove.

Hot mantle material rises in a column called a **heat plume**. This heat plume rises toward an ocean ridge. When it reaches the base of the plate above, the hot material flows horizontally. The comparative coolness of the plate above gradually cools the magma in the current. The magma descends again below a subduction zone. That's basic science: warm air or liquid rises; cool air or liquid falls. The tectonic plate is dragged along as the heated material moves horizontally.

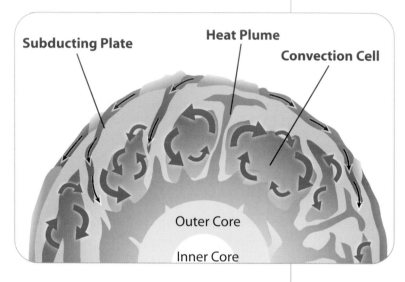

More recently, geologists have suggested that, yes, there are convection cells in the mantle. They also suggest, though, that these convection cells probably would not exert sufficient force to move the plates. Geologists now think that plates are moved by a combination of a push from the material spreading out at ridges, and a pull exerted by seafloor material subducting at a trench. This has been called "ridge-push and slab-pull."

Island Arcs and Hot Spots

Heat plumes within the mantle play a role in its movement. They also play a role in the development of land itself. They do this by causing volcanoes to form. As we saw earlier, volcanoes often erupt near subduction zones. Volcanoes generally form along the curve of a trench. When these volcanoes form in an ocean, they are called **island arcs**.

Island arcs have been formed throughout Earth's history. When island-arc crust approaches a subduction zone, the seafloor returns to the mantle. But the island-arc crust, which is less dense, is pushed up against the continental crust and may attach to it. Much of the land that became part of the original North American continent was probably formed as island arcs. The Aleutian Islands off Alaska are an island arc.

Hot spots are places in the mantle where heat plumes rise. The hot spots rise through the lithosphere, instead of at the edge of a tectonic plate. Magma is forced onto the surface as lava. Lava builds up, forming new mountains. The plate over the hot spot continues to move, but the location of the hot spot in the mantle does not. That means that older mountains move away from the hot spot, while newer ones form. If these mountains reach above sea level, they form a line of visible islands. The Hawaiian Islands were formed by a hot spot under the Pacific plate.

Hot spots can also be under continental land. Yellowstone National Park is located over a hot spot. Geysers of various sizes and boiling-hot mineral springs abound throughout the park, giving the beautiful scenery much of its attraction.

An island arc is a chain of volcanoes that forms as a result of seafloor descending into a trench. Rising heat causes lava to flow.

Continent

Island Arc Volcanoes

Trench

Oceanic Crust

The Aleutian Islands (photographed from space) formed as a volcanic island arc along a subduction zone in the northern Pacific.

Chapter 4

Rocks and Mountains —Made and Remade

Tectonic plates are made of rock. Rock is defined as a mass of solid mineral matter. That mineral matter is the main solid stuff of the planet. Several thousand minerals have been identified. Most of them came from within the earth.

Magma makes up only about 5 percent of the mantle. It is that part of the mantle that can become molten. When magma flows out onto the planet's surface, it is called lava. The other 95 percent of the mantle material consists of minerals, as well as rocks formed out of minerals.

The Rock Cycle

There are three main types of rocks. Igneous rocks are those that have hardened directly from magma. They may have hardened within the mantle or crust. They then may be carried to the surface. Or, they may harden from lava that flows on the surface.

Once igneous rocks are exposed to air and water, they quickly break down into sediments. Sediments are the crumbs of rocks. They are eroded by water and wind. They are then carried into low places, especially by and into water. As more and more layers, or strata, of sediment are added above, sediments below eventually harden into rock. Rock formed in this way is called sedimentary rock.

Either igneous or sedimentary rock can be buried deep in the earth. This is where pressure and heat from the mantle metamorphose, or change, them. Their minerals recrystallize and form different kinds of rocks. These rocks are categorized as metamorphic rocks.

The Rock Cycle

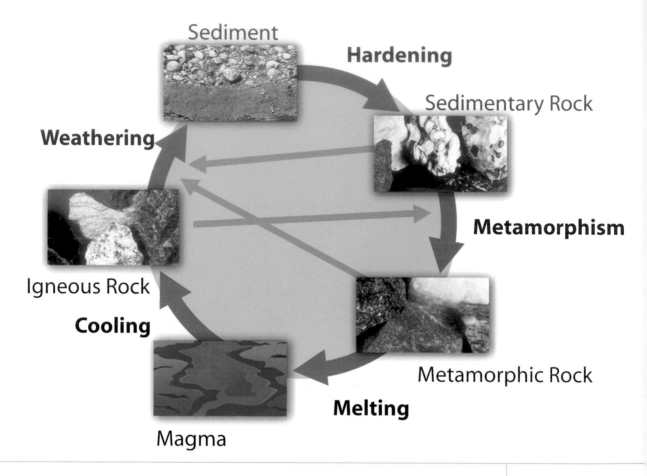

Sediment

Hardening

Sedimentary Rock

Weathering

Igneous Rock

Cooling

Magma

Metamorphism

Metamorphic Rock

Melting

Granite is a common igneous rock. Several other similar rocks are also formed directly from magma. Together these rocks are called granitic. Granitic rocks are **intrusive**. This means that they cooled and crystallized beneath the planet's surface, but they were eventually uplifted to the surface. Much of the exposed rock of North America is granitic. Stone Mountain in Georgia is a huge single dome of granite. British Columbia has vast expanses of exposed granitic rock. The presidential figures on Mount Rushmore in the Black Hills of South Dakota were carved out of granite that was formed 1.7 billion years ago.

Georgia's Stone Mountain is one of the world's largest pieces of granite. It formed underground about 300 million years ago. Then the crust above it eroded away.

Intrusive igneous rock and lava are different from each other. Intrusive igneous rock cooled and crystallized below the surface. It formed when magma entered an area where the temperature was comparatively cool. Lava rock, on the other hand, is **extrusive**. It was spewed onto the surface by a volcano. The lava then hardened and crystallized. Several different kinds of extrusive rocks may be formed in lava.

The Bottom of the Canyon

About 3,500 feet (1,067 m) down in Arizona's Grand Canyon, the visible rock is very dark. This dark rock is called Vishnu schist. It is a metamorphic rock that was formed from earlier sedimentary and igneous rock. It was once the root of a vast mountain system that formed about 1.7 billion years ago. The mountains have since eroded away. The area was covered many times by seas. This added new layers of sediment over the Vishnu schist. In addition, about 1.4 billion years ago, the Vishnu schist was intruded by an igneous rock called Zoroaster granite.

Seeing Precambrian Rocks
in a Geology Museum

It's helpful to visit a geology museum to compare samples of the different kinds of rock. Shown here are some common rock types. Because rock type alone does not indicate its age, any or all of these rocks could be Precambrian, Paleozoic, Mesozoic, or Cenozoic. They can be identified by their simple, visible characteristics such as texture (size of grains), color (dark or light), and type of layering (if any).

Intrusive Igneous Rocks

<u>granite</u> ↘
large crystals easily seen,
light colored

↙ <u>gabbro</u>
large crystals,
dark colored

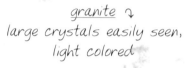

Extrusive Igneous Rocks

<u>basalt</u> ↘
magnification needed to
see the small crystals,
dark colored

<u>obsidian</u> ↘
no crystals,
glassy

↙ <u>pumice</u>
frothy texture,
tiny air spaces,
light colored

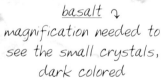

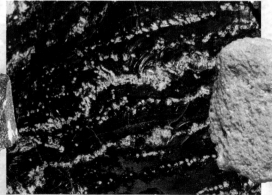

Sedimentary Rocks

shale ↘
very tiny particles
in thin layer

sandstone
↘ grains of sand
cemented together

↳ _conglomerate_
grains larger than sand
cemented together

↳ _limestone_
reacts with acid

Metamorphic Rocks

↘ _slate_
similar to shale, but splits into
flat sheets

schist ↗
coarse grained,
splits into
flaky slabs

↘ _quartzite_
similar to sandstone, but
with grains fused (not
cemented) together

↘ _marble_
no layers, reacts
with acid

↳ _gneiss_
large crystals,
banded

41

Defining Volcanoes

Volcanoes are places in the earth's crust where magma oozes onto the surface. Most volcanoes we know today are mountains that have been formed from lava. The lava continually built up as it cooled. Most of these volcanic mountains later had their vents, or openings, closed off from their magma chambers. They became inactive.

There are probably as many as 1,300 volcanoes on Earth that could become active again. North America has such volcanoes in Alaska, Washington, Mexico, and Iceland. The state of Hawaii (which is not part of North America) also has active volcanoes.

Volcanoes are often defined by the kind of extrusive igneous rock they were formed from, which determines how resistant to flow the lava is. The amount of silica and oxygen in the magma determines how **viscous** the lava is. Viscosity determines the kind of volcano formed.

North America experienced a basalt flow about 17 million years ago. The basalt now covers the Columbia River region of Washington and Oregon.

Not all volcanic action forms mountains. Throughout the history of the planet, there has been occasional massive oozing from great cracks in the crust. This oozing produced rocks called **flood basalts**. The oldest flood basalt identified by scientists was formed 3.9 billion years ago.

Another flood basalt formed when the Atlantic Ocean basin started to open up. This began the breakup of supercontinent Pangea, about 200 million years ago. At that time, flood basalts formed all along the edges of the supercontinent. Because basalt can flow a long distance before hardening, it can form **shield volcanoes**, which are generally low and broad. Hawaii's big volcanoes are shield volcanoes.

↳ *Snow-covered Mount Hood, a composite volcano bigger than many shields*

Stratovolcanoes are steeper and cone-shaped. They are produced by the igneous rock called **andesite**. After an eruption begins (usually explosively), andesite travels down the side of a volcano quite slowly. It doesn't go far before hardening. The lava quickly breaks up into chunks. Stratovolcanoes are also called **composite volcanoes** because they are often made up of alternating layers of lava and ash.

The third kind of volcano can be called a dome. It is composed of the rock **rhyolite**, which is too sticky to flow. Rhyolite mounds up around the vent of the volcano.

↳ *The long, low form of a shield volcano in the Pacific*

Sometimes **cinder cones** are called volcanoes. Cinder cones are steep-sided cones of basaltic cinders that has exploded from a vent. They often form on the side of a large shield volcano when a new vent opens.

A lava dome has formed within the collapsed top of Mount St. Helens in Washington. →

Where Volcanoes Form

Volcanoes can form wherever there is a weak spot or break in the crust. Most of them, however, form along the margins of tectonic plates.

Ocean-ridge volcanoes form the ocean ridges where new crustal material rises from the mantle. Most of these volcanoes form beneath the surface of the sea. However, Iceland's volcanoes are ocean-ridge volcanoes.

Island-arc volcanoes form rows of islands in the ocean. These rows are parallel to a trench where oceanic crust is being subducted beneath continental crust. The Aleutians, located off Alaska, and the West Indies in the Caribbean, are island arcs.

Hot-spot volcanoes occur away from a plate margin. They are formed over a long period of time as the plate moves over the hot spot in the mantle. The Hawaiian Islands were formed by a hot-spot volcano. The active volcanoes on the big island of Hawaii are gigantic shield volcanoes.

Continental-margin volcanoes occur where seafloor material is being subducted and some of the melted material comes to the surface.

↳ *A volcano erupting in the island arc of the Caribbean*

The Ring of Fire

There are subduction zones along the whole outer edge of the Pacific Ocean. These stretch from both the Pacific plate and two smaller plates next to Central and South America. Volcanoes flourish along these plate boundaries. These volcanoes create a pattern that is often called the Ring of Fire. More than half the world's active volcanoes and numerous earthquakes take place in the Ring of Fire.

The huge Andes range that runs the length of South America was created in this way. In North America, the movement of the little Juan de Fuca plate along British Columbia, Washington, and Oregon causes volcanic activity along the plate margin, especially in the Cascade Mountains.

Finally, continental-rift volcanoes occur where two sections of continent are separating. The main example today is the Great Rift Valley in East Africa. The Red Sea is part of this rift.

When Land Meets Land

New Scientist magazine said in 2002, "If it's a truly majestic mountain range you're after, you can't beat crashing a couple of tectonic plates together. The faster the collision and the stronger the rock, the bigger the peaks produced." The writer probably had in mind the Himalayas, which resulted when the Indian plate crashed into the Asian plate. Many earlier mountains ranges were formed in the same way.

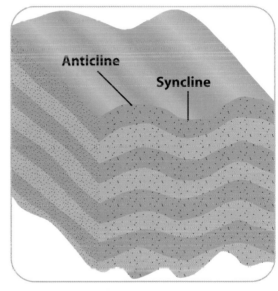

Two important movements of Earth's crust form mountains during the collision of tectonic plates. These two movements produce folds and faults. Both are produced by stress in the crustal rock.

Folding might also be called crumpling. When a force is exerted on layers of rock, the layers might just bend. They compress into wave-like patterns. Imagine you are pushing a tablecloth into a series of arches and valleys. Folds can be so small that there is no elevation in the land above them to indicate that folds lie below. Folds can also be huge, raising vast ranges of mountains. The photo on pages 36 and 37 shows folded rock.

Basically, folds are of two kinds. The two usually occur together in together. An **anticline** is the arched part of a fold. A **syncline** is the dip of the fold. Rock can be so deformed during a collision that the folded structure is turned vertically.

Driving Through Sidling Hill Road Cut

Rock structures called synclines are important evidence of the bending forces that rock layers have gone through in the past. West of Hancock, Maryland, part of a hill was dynamited away to make way for U.S. Highway 68. An almost perfect syncline can be seen in the side of the road cut. In a nearby visitor center, exhibits explain the geology of the syncline, along with other interesting facts of the surrounding area.

This syncline is one of a group of folds in the rock of the area. They produced a series of parallel ridges and valleys. The syncline, like those in the other ridges, is made of sandstone that is very resistant to erosion. The valleys between the ridges were worn low, because they were made of rock that is less resistant to erosion.

If the stress on rock becomes too great, it may bend too much. It then breaks, or fractures. When the two sides of the rock on each side of a fracture move relative to each other, the change, or **deformation**, is called a fault. Faults are named by the way they move.

Many fractures occur at an angle to the surface. When the section below an angled fracture moves upward compared to rock on the other side of the fracture, the fault is called a normal fault. A normal fault is no more "normal" than other kinds of faults. "Normal" is an old name miners used. Normal faulting formed the Grand Teton Mountains in Wyoming. The western part of the land, beneath the fault, rose in a huge block, while the eastern part dropped.

In a reverse fault, the opposite is true— the rock above the fracture rises up the slope. A thrust fault is a type of reverse fault in which the angle of the fracture is quite shallow.

In a lateral fault (also called strike-slip fault), the rock doesn't fracture at an angle. Instead the fracture is vertical, and the two blocks slide past each other.

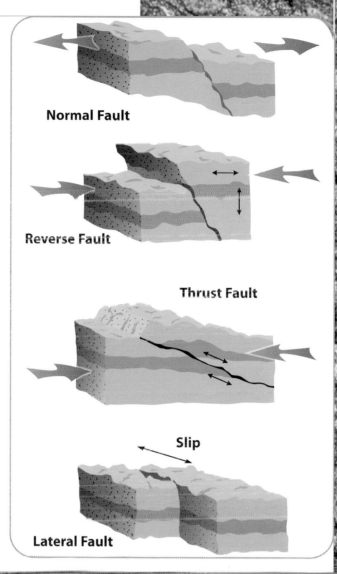

Normal Fault

Reverse Fault

Thrust Fault

Slip

Lateral Fault

The red circle highlights a reverse fault visible in this hillside. ↪

↰ *Large-scale faulting of crustal rock can create spectacular mountains like the Grand Tetons, or it can be an earthquake that harms people.*

An earthquake in California made this highway section collapse. ↱

Earthquakes

Earth's rock is always settling or moving slightly. As we saw on page 21, the vibrations given off by the movement of rock are recorded by seismographs. If the movement causes rock to break, the event is an earthquake. Quakes may be so deep or slight that they are not noticed by people. Or they may be so strong that they destroy buildings and even rearrange the land.

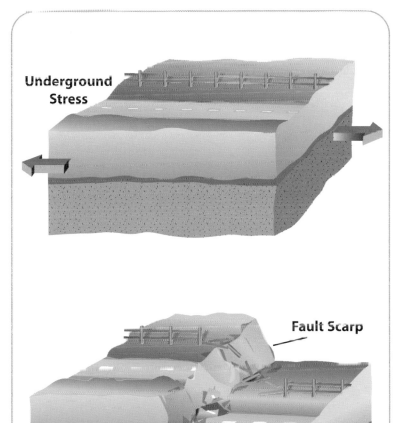

Underground Stress

Fault Scarp

Epicenter

Fault Plane

At the end of 2004, an earthquake occurred in the oceanic crust off the coast of Sumatra, in the huge island nation of Indonesia. It measured 9.0 on the Richter Scale (see page 51) and was the second largest earthquake ever recorded. The quake set off a giant ocean wave, called a **tsunami** (tsu-NAM-ee) that rushed across the low-lying islands and coastal areas of eleven nations. More than 225,000 people died in the powerful wave and millions more were left homeless.

↩ *An earthquake occurs when stresses in the rock of the crust become so overwhelming that the rock breaks, or faults. The stress-relieving movement can be up and down or sideways.*

Quake Lake

In 1959, an earthquake hit southwestern Montana. It was the largest in the history of the state, which rarely feels earthquakes. Aftershocks were felt for several months. The quake produced many **fault scarps**. These are cliffs formed by faulting or fracturing of the earth's crust. Most of the deaths caused by the quake resulted from campers being buried by a massive landslide that was triggered by the earthquake.

The landslide came from a steep valley wall along the Madison River. The rock material in the slide dammed the river. This created a new lake, which has been named Quake Lake. Trees that once grew in the valley of the river are now stumps projecting from the lake. The road running through the river valley was badly damaged by scarps. In other places, the lake submerged the road. The landslide scar is easily seen at one end of the lake.

landslide

HOW DO THEY KNOW
How Strong an Earthquake Is?

Scientists indicate the strength of an earthquake mainly by the damage it does. They use a scale called the Richter Scale named for California's Charles Richter, who developed the scale in 1935. Each number is ten times greater than the previous number in the movement of a seismometer in reaction to a seismic wave.

- 1 to 3: Recorded on local seismographs, but not generally felt
- 3 to 4: May be felt, but no damage done
- 5: Felt widely, but little damage except near the epicenter of quake
- 6: Damage to poorly constructed buildings within a few miles of the epicenter
- 7: Serious damage up to 60 miles (100 km) of epicenter
- 8: These are the "great" earthquakes with serious damage and many deaths over several hundred miles
- 9: Very rare "great" earthquakes with terrible destruction up to 1,000 miles (1,600 km)

In the last few years, scientists have used the Global Positioning System (GPS) of satellites to measure actual earth movements. See page 61.

After an earthquake, the earth continues to vibrate for quite a while. Some of the vibrations may be large enough to be called aftershocks. In 1995, Kobe, Japan, experienced a severe earthquake that killed 5,000 people. Those left alive experienced a frightening 716 aftershocks during the next 24 hours after the quake.

Folding and faulting are the main events that occur in rock. The ups and downs, from the highest mountains to the lowest valleys, with vast plains in between, are what make the basic structure of the scenery around us. But what we see around us is only the most recent of the structure changes that have gone on in North America.

Chapter 5

The Heart of North America

The oldest and most stable part of a continent is called its **craton**. This is the part formed during Precambrian times. Later, other landmasses **accreted**, or attached, to it. Some continents have more than one craton. Layers of sedimentary rock usually cover these.

In general, the oldest rocks on Earth are the deepest. However, geologists can rarely reach far enough into the crust of the planet to study these rocks. Fortunately, Earth itself sometimes lets scientists peer into the past, and even into the earth itself. This is because a large part of North America's craton has been exposed.

During the Ice Age of the last 2 million years, a great ice sheet crept down from the Arctic. This ice sheet spread over much of North America. As it moved, the force of the moving ice swept younger rock from the craton. The part of North America that was exposed, or made visible above the earth's surface, is called the **Canadian Shield**. The oldest known rocks that have been discovered are located in the Canadian Shield.

The Canadian Shield covers about 1.8 million square miles (4.8 million sq km). The part of the craton that is not exposed above the earth's surface is called the North American **platform**. Geologists have never had a good look at North America's platform because it lies too deep under newer rock.

↶ *Throughout most of time, the North American craton (shield and platform) lay along the equator. The familiar shape shown here did not exist until recent times.*

Shield

Platform

Shield

EQUATOR - - - - - - - - - - - - - - - - - - **EQUATOR**

Platform

Shield

↶ *The ancient rock of North America's craton is visible in the Canadian Shield, where later rock was scraped off.*

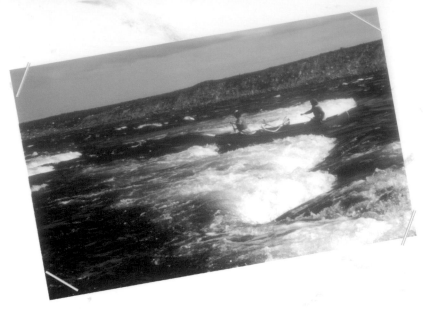

Canoeing Across the Canadian Shield

The Canadian Shield covers most of Central and Eastern Canada, along with a portion of the United States in the Great Lakes region. The soil layer that has developed over the Precambrian bedrock is very thin. This means any granite, gneiss, and other crystalline rocks that make up the craton can be seen.

Adventurous people enjoy canoe trips across the shield. They travel on the many interconnecting lakes and streams. Rivers cut through the rock, forming rapids. Canoers have to portage, or carry their canoes, across expanses of exposed rock.

Much of the shield is covered with evergreen forests. The northern portion is **tundra**, treeless land that remains frozen underground, as in the photo below. Abundant wildlife is usually visible along the way.

When the North American craton was first formed, the land had massive mountains. The Archean rock of these mountains eroded away. The eroded material filled in the valleys and formed new sedimentary rock. Both the old rock and the new were folded. This folding formed twisted masses that further thickened the crust. Today, the Canadian Shield is fairly flat, with no major mountain ranges. Its highest point has an elevation of only about 1,650 feet (500 m).

Gold, silver, zinc, and copper are pure metallic elements that are mined today on the Canadian Shield. This is because they were brought up to the surface in magma long ago. The Precambrian rocks of the Canadian Shield contain deposits of the **ores** of iron, copper, nickel, and other metals. Many of these deposits are among the richest in the world.

Iron ores mined from the Canadian Shield: hematite (left) and magnetite (right), which is magnetic

Pure metallic elements mined from the Canadian Shield: gold, shownattached to quartz (left), copper (above), and silver (right)

Assembling the Craton

The North American craton was built from six (some geologists say seven) landmasses called **microcontinents**. These were formed between 3 and 2.5 billion years ago. Each of them has a structure and history that are different from the others. This makes each microcontinent easy to identify.

Starting about 2 billion years ago, these microcontinents moved northward. They crashed into each other and remain attached. Together, they formed one new continent that geologists call **Laurentia**.

↺ *Several ancient microcontinents joined up and became the original craton of North America, shown here against the outline of today's continent.*

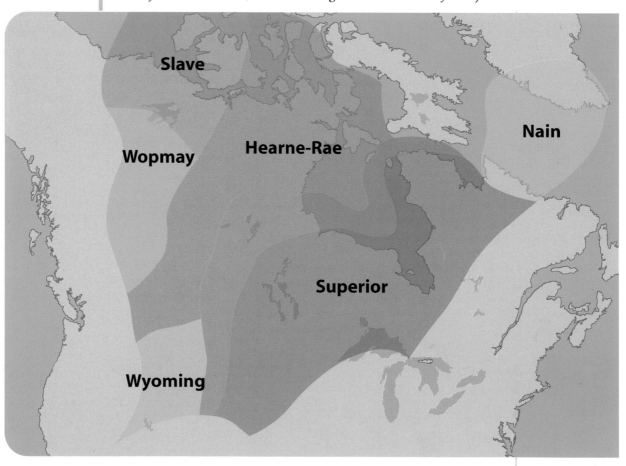

This granite in Ontario, Canada, is part of the Superior Province of the North American craton.

Geologists have given the six pieces of crust, which they called **provinces** of our craton, the names of Slave, Nain, Superior, Wyoming, Hearne, and Rae. Hearne and Rae are sometimes regarded as a single province—the Hearne Rae or Churchill. Wopmay is thought to be the seventh province.

The largest part of the North American craton is the Superior Province. It stretches from the Arctic down into Minnesota. Superior Province is about 1,500 miles (2,400 km) wide. It includes about one-quarter of all exposed Archean crust in the world.

Superior is not one solid piece of granite. Instead, it consists of many different belts of rock, called **terranes,** that joined up during the Archean Eon. The different belts, in general, line up from northeast to southwest. They probably originated separately. Some were island arcs, produced by volcanoes. Some might have been sediments from times when the margin of the province was inactive. However they originated, they all ended up together as the Superior Province.

Forming strips within the granite of the Superior Province are different rocks called greenstone belts. These belts formed from lava between 3 and 2.7 billion years ago. They frequently contain chlorite, which is a greenish mineral. One of the largest of these greenstone belts is located between the Great Lakes and James Bay.

Rocks called greenstones made belts within Superior Province almost 3 billion years ago.

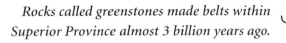

Diamonds are found in both Slave Province and a province in India. Perhaps they were once connected.

Slave Province, which is much smaller than Superior, is located in the western part of the craton. It joined the Superior Province about 2.5 billion years ago. The Slave Province contains the oldest rocks discovered on Earth. These rocks are about 4.03 billion years old. One Canadian scientist, Wouter Bleeker, of the Geological Survey of Canada, suggested that other parts of the same microcontinent that produced the Slave Province are now found in India, Zimbabwe, and the United States. Interestingly, both the Indian province and Slave Province produce diamonds.

Nain Province is a small area that forms the southern tip of Greenland. It includes rocks older than 3.8 billion years. These rocks have been highly metamorphosed (changed by heat and pressure). By 2.6 billion years ago, Nain Province was complete.

The province attached itself to the northern end of the Superior Province about 1.8 billion years ago. At some time after that, Europe started to move away from North America. It tried to take Greenland with it. The movement failed to take the island very far. It did leave Greenland separated from the mainland of Canada by the Labrador Sea and Davis Strait, however. Today, most of Greenland's Nain rock is covered by an ice sheet except along the coast.

The coastal valleys called fjords cut deeply into the Nain rock of Greenland's southern coast.

The Hearne, Rae, and Wyoming provinces of Archean rock were added to the craton during the Early Proterozoic Eon. These parts collided, forming twisted mountain chains. These chains built up a huge area of the craton west of the Superior Province. Soon after, the Wopmay, a fairly old piece of crust that is often called the seventh microcontinent, collided with the Slave Province and remained attached.

During the next 200 million years, two large belts were added across the south. These belts make up most of what is the southern half of the United States today. The longest Precambrian mountain belt is called the Grenville. It collided with the eastern side of the Superior Province about 1.1 billion years ago. The Grenville Province is about 1,250 miles (2,000 km) long and up to 375 miles (600 km) wide. It runs from Mexico, attaching to the slightly older Mazatzal belt, all the way north to Newfoundland. There is a break in the belt, caused by the Ouachita Mountains in Alabama and Arkansas.

↰ *The rocky coast of Newfoundland is the northern end of the Grenville Province, which attached itself to the craton about 1.1 million years ago.*

The Grenville Province was the last of the landmasses added to the North American craton. It was added by collisions that took place in Precambrian times and remained attached. Other pieces were later accreted as smaller fragments. This means that a chunk of crust hit another chunk and they remained stuck together. Even with all this land added, though, North America still didn't look much like the continent of today. In later periods of Earth history, more pieces would be added.

Early Supercontinents

Alfred Wegener thought that all of today's continents were once part of the 200-million-year-old supercontinent he called Pangea. Today's scientists speculate that there were two earlier supercontinents, both in Precambrian times. The North American craton was part of these supercontinents.

Many of the chunks of crust that moved around during the early Precambrian times were large enough to be called microcontinents. It is probable that at least three-quarters of the rock that later became the cratons of the continents was formed during this period.

Forces within the planet moved the chunks of crust around randomly, without a set pattern. If you have ever ridden in bumper cars at a carnival, you know that sometimes your car is alone. Then, perhaps just seconds later, you seem to be caught in a traffic jam, with many cars all running into each other. That's the way the continents moved around in the past. They didn't move fast, since plates move at a rate of only a couple of inches a year. Those inches added up, however, to continuous movement across the mantle.

By sheer chance, the continental landmasses came to collide with each other about 1.1 billion years ago. They formed one vast continent. It stretched from pole to pole and lay in one vast sea. This supercontinent has been given the name Rodinia, which is Russian for "motherland." A single ocean, called the Iapetus Ocean, surrounded it. Rodinia lasted until about 700 million years ago.

The small continental mass making up what would become North America is called Laurentia, after the Laurentian Mountains of Canada. Laurentia was probably located in the middle of Rodinia, lying along the equator. The supercontinent began to break up about 750 million years ago.

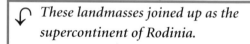

These landmasses joined up as the supercontinent of Rodinia.

HOW DO THEY KNOW
How Fast the Plates Move?

Actual movement of the tectonic plates can be determined now by GPS, the Global Positioning System. This is the same satellite system that is used to locate cars on the move, sailboats at sea, or even hikers in the woods.

Radio signals are continually sent by orbiting satellites to receivers on the ground. A receiver may be in a car, on a building, or in a hiker's backpack. The distance from each of several satellites to the receiver is slightly different. Radio signals take slightly different times to reach it. A computer at the receiving station can accurately pinpoint where the signals intersect. It can show the location of the receiver within millimeters. The GPS system indicates that the North American plate is moving northeastward at about 2 inches (5 cm) a year.

Satellite One

Satellite Two

Satellite Three

Geologists in the field using Global Positioning System receivers to determine their exact location

Since the 1990s, many geologists have begun to think that another supercontinent existed after Rodinia and before Pangea. It was given the name Pannotia. It is also sometimes referred to as the Vendian supercontinent. *Vendian* is a name sometimes used for the Late Proterozoic period, from about 1 billion years ago to the end of Precambrian times, 543 million years ago.

After Rodinia broke apart, each of two main parts were, for a "short" time, near one of Earth's poles. Laurentia was near the South Pole. Earth's continents went through a glacial period, when ice covered large parts of the planet. When **glaciers** melt, they leave behind deposits of rocks that the moving ice has scraped off the rock beneath.

Glacial deposits from that period are found in a belt lying approximately from today's Rocky Mountains in the United States to the Arctic. A similar band of glacial deposits from that same time period follows the East Coast.

↺ *These landmasses joined up as the supercontinent of Pannotia.*

The two parts of Rodinia gradually met again south of the equator. They linked up with Africa and became the new supercontinent called Pannotia. Pannotia remained wrapped around the South Pole. But it split into several parts, including Laurentia (which moved north of the equator), Gondwana, and Baltica. Baltica became most of northern Europe.

The landmass that was gradually evolving into North America underwent many changes in Precambrian times. But the rocky heart of our continent was not the only thing that was evolving. In the vast ocean that covered much of the planet, living things were getting a strong start. They were developing, changing, and multiplying into the life we know today.

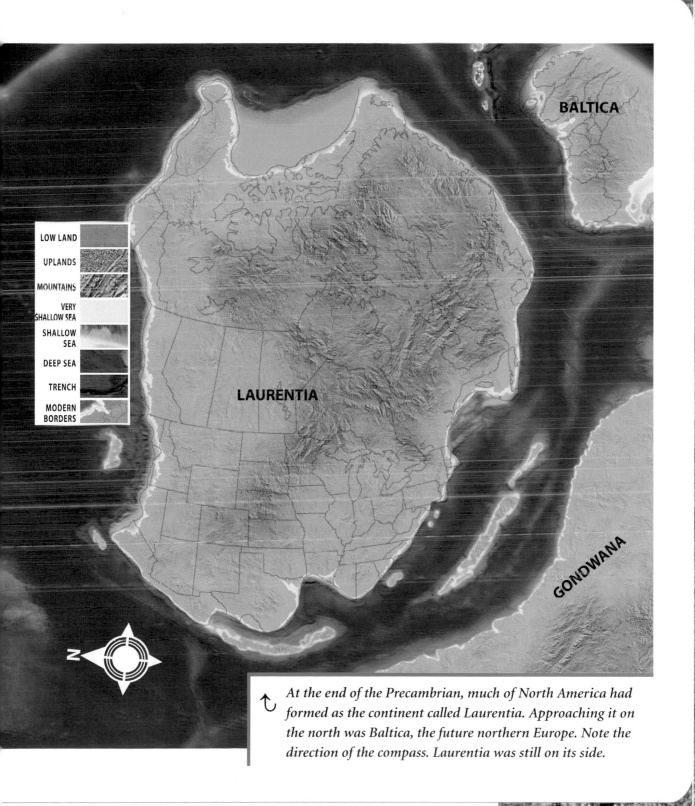

BALTICA

LOW LAND

UPLANDS

MOUNTAINS

VERY
SHALLOW SEA

SHALLOW
SEA

DEEP SEA

TRENCH

MODERN
BORDERS

LAURENTIA

GONDWANA

N

At the end of the Precambrian, much of North America had formed as the continent called Laurentia. Approaching it on the north was Baltica, the future northern Europe. Note the direction of the compass. Laurentia was still on its side.

Chapter 6

The Beginnings of Living Things

Naturalists were certain that living things had just begun to flourish after the Precambrian ended. They located numerous fossils of shelled animals called **trilobites**, as well as some other primitive animals. They used the differences in these animals, and the rock layers in which they were found, to create timetables of geologic history.

More recently, however, techniques for locating and dating organic (living) material have improved. Now paleontologists see that about 85 percent of the evolution of living things took place before the Cambrian Period started, especially among microscopic, single-celled creatures. It is almost impossible to locate fossils of these microbes. This is because the marks these one-celled creatures left in stone may look no different than marks left through other causes.

The first traces of fossils that might have been living organisms are found in rocks from the earliest times. These traces consist of carbon that is different from the carbon in other nearby rocks. However, there is no way to tell if this carbon was from once-living creatures or not.

The New and the Old

Throughout most of science history, living things were divided into plant and animal kingdoms. Then, in the 1960s, biologists evaluated all they knew so far. They came to realize that **fungi**, **bacteria**, and **protists** (such as protozoa and most **algae**) did not really fit into either the plant or the animal kingdom. They soon divided living things into five separate kingdoms: plants, animals, fungi, protists, and prokaryotes, which are a type of bacteria that do not have a nucleus in the cells.

These odd round shapes in the Precambrian rock of Glacier National Park are **stromatolites**. Such layered structures are thought to be evidence of very early living things, called **cyanobacteria**.

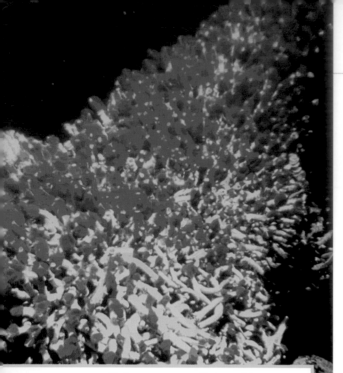

Tubeworms are living things that do not need oxygen. They live off bacteria in the extreme heat of ocean floor vents. ↰

In the 1970s, biologists determined that yet another category was needed. Called **archaea**, these are living cells unlike any other bacteria. Because they are capable of living in extremely poisonous and hot settings, some biologists call them "extremophiles."

Archaea were found in the poisonous hot springs of Yellowstone National Park and deep in petroleum deposits. They were also found in the oxygen-free mud of holes in the ocean floor. Traces of fossil archaea have been found in the rocks of the Isua district of west Greenland. These traces have been dated to 3.8 billion years old. They are the oldest living things identified.

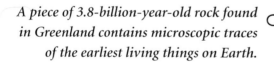

A piece of 3.8-billion-year-old rock found in Greenland contains microscopic traces of the earliest living things on Earth. ↱

The Puzzling Stromatolites

Stromatolites are layered limestone structures. They have been described as looking like wrinkled pancakes. They formed carpets on the floor of ancient seas. Stromatolites appear to be made by colonies of algae and cyanobacteria (formerly called blue-green algae).

These colonies formed reefs the way coral does today, and they also carried out the process of **photosynthesis**. They can combine carbon dioxide and water to produce food. A waste product of the process is oxygen. This oxygen accumulated and rose out of the seawater. It gradually formed an oxygen-rich atmosphere for our planet.

The oldest stromatolites known were found in Australia. They have been dated to 3.4 billion years ago. For well over 2 billion years, stromatolites were the main form of life on the planet. Their fossils are found in many rocks. A major belt of rock formed by stromatolites in Ontario, Canada, was formed 2.7 billion years ago.

The Gunflint Formation, also in Ontario, is located in Archean rocks just south of Hudson Bay. The fossils there are so small that they can be identified only through a microscope. Known as microfossils, they have been dated as 2.1 billion years old.

Stromatolites are not just things of the ancient past. They are still formed in a few sites in Australia and the Bahamas in the Caribbean. They consist of various single-celled organisms, such as cyanobacteria and purple sulfur bacteria, within limestone rock.

A museum exhibit shows what scientists think the scene would have been like when stromatolites (the round objects in the bottom half of the picture) formed in Precambrian shallow seas.

Ancient Rocks along Going-to-the-Sun Highway

Going-to-the-Sun highway runs east-west across the mountains of Glacier National Park in Montana. It begins in the heavily forested areas and rises up into the mountain tundra. These are treeless plains where the soil underground never thaws. The road is patched in many places where landslides and snow avalanches have damaged it.

The sequence of rock is unusual here. This is because the older rock layers are found on top of the younger ones. This happened because a fault carried a block of Precambrian rock up and over rock that was formed during the Mesozoic Era. Erosion, primarily by streams and glaciers, carved these rock layers into their present shape.

Large amounts of lime, sand, and mud went into making this Precambrian rock. Most of the marks in the rock show events from the Precambrian. For example, there are many ripple marks, such as might have formed in shallow water. There are signs of life, too. Fossil stromatolites are seen in limestone along the road.

The sandstones and mudstones vary in color, including gray, green, brown, and red. The color differences are due mostly to the variety and amount of iron minerals in the rock.

In the 1990s, geologists began to question whether all of these odd formations had anything to do with living things. It seems that stromatolites can form from limestone on the seafloor without any help from living organisms. The geologists speculate that any fossilized microbes found in stromatolites may have just been along for the ride. They were not creators of the ride itself. The puzzle has not been solved.

Oxygen, Iron, and Living Things

The amount of oxygen in Earth's atmosphere increased sharply about 2.3 billion years ago. Scientists know this because of the appearance of banded iron formations around the world. Banded iron is made up of alternating layers of an iron oxide mineral such as hematite or magnetite and a silicon oxide, such as **chert**. The mining of these ancient formations today supplies most of the iron used around the world.

The earliest rocks contained a great deal of iron. As these rocks eroded, the iron entered seawater as **ions**. Ions are incomplete atoms that easily react with other elements, especially oxygen. As photosynthetic cyanobacteria developed in the water, they gave off oxygen. The oxygen chemically reacted with the iron, forming iron oxides. The iron oxides dropped as solid bits to the ocean floor, where they collected.

Iron ore is removed from huge open-pit mines, such as this one in Minnesota. The iron was accumulated with the help of living things.

The iron content of the rock called banded iron may reflect changing environments for early, very primitive living things.

When there was no longer enough iron available to use up the oxygen, the oxygen levels may have become poisonous. The cyanobacteria population dropped. While cyanobacteria were reestablishing themselves, the silica layer built up. Later, the cyanobacteria were plentiful again. They could produce enough oxygen to build up another band of iron oxides. And so this alternating process continued for millions of years.

An Ancestor of Today's Animals

Living things remained single-celled for hundreds of millions of years. They reproduced by duplicating themselves. About 1 billion years ago, however, these cells developed nuclei. The nucleus of a living cell contains **genetic** information. Multicellular creatures developed, with the ability to reproduce by combining cells from two different organisms.

Over the last few years of the Precambrian, living things that can be identified as animal also appeared. Unlike plant cells, animal cells do not have tough, semi-rigid walls that limit or constrain the shape of the cells. A few of these earliest animals have been preserved.

These puzzling fossils are called Ediacaran life, after the Ediacara Hills of Australia. These first signs of a fairly complex animal life were found in these hills in 1946. The soft-bodied organisms that left these strange fossils apparently appeared on the scene starting about 650 million years ago and lasted only through the remainder of the Precambrian.

The Ediacaran fossils look sort of like worms, sort of like jellyfish, sort of like corals. No one knows, though, whether these were the forerunners of today's animals. Perhaps they were "failed experiments" of evolution. Few Ediacaran fossils have been found later than Precambrian rocks.

Ediacaran animals, shown here in a museum display, disappeared by the end of Precambrian times.

Ediacaran-type fossils have now been found in about thirty locations around the planet. Certain rocks in the Mackenzie Mountains in the Northwest Territories of Canada contain the largest collection of Ediacaran fossils in the world.

The Scene is Set

The fossils of living things found in Precambrian rocks are few and far between. Few of them resemble the living things known today. And yet, the scene was set for what has been called the greatest evolutionary event in Earth's history.

After Precambrian time ended about 543 million years ago, the next geologic time period would be the Cambrian Period, starting the Paleozoic Era. During the Cambrian "Explosion of Life," the ancestors of all of today's living things appeared on the scene and began to evolve.

The scene was set, too, for the building of a North America that would be more recognizable to people today. About 75 percent of the continental crust had been formed. Laurentia had a stable heart on which new lands would grow during later eras. The continent continued its own movement across the face of planet Earth.

GEOLOGIC TIME SCALE

Time Period	Tectonic Events	Biological Events
Hadean Eon *4.5–3.96 billion years ago* Named for Hades, or Hell	No Earth rocks from this time found	None
Archean Eon *3.96–2.5 billion years ago* Name means "Ancient"	Oldest known rocks First permanent crust First stable continents	Seawater formed First bacteria Atmosphere formed
Proterozoic Eon *2.5 billion–543 million*	North American craton formed First iron–bearing sediments First large glaciation Formation and breakup of Rodinia supercontinent Gondwana, southern supercontinent, formed	Free oxygen in atmosphere First nucleated cells, allowing sexual reproduction First multicellular animals First animals with exoskeletons First fungi

PHANEROZOIC TIME • 543 million years ago to present

PALEOZOIC ERA • 543 to 248 million years ago

Time Period	Tectonic Events	Biological Events
Cambrian Period *543–248 million years ago* Named for old name of Wales	Laurentia separated from Siberia	Cambrian Explosion: Major diversification of marine invertebrates
Ordovician Period *490–443 million years ago* Named for a Celtic tribe in Wales	First Iapetus Ocean Taconic orogeny in northeastern Laurentia	First true vertebrates: jawless fish First land plants Mass extinction
Silurian Period *443–417 million years ago* Named for a Celtic tribe in Wales	Caledonian orogeny Shallow seas on Laurentia	First vascular plants First insects First jawed fish
Devonian Period *417–354 million years ago* Named for Devon, England	Major reef building	First forests First seed–baring plants First four–footed animals First amphibians
CARBONIFEROUS PERIOD 354 to 290 million years ago — **Mississippian Epoch** *354–323 million years ago* Named for Mississippi River Valley	Antler orogeny	Ferns abundant First land vertebrates
Pennsylvanian Epoch *323–290 million years ago* Named for coal formations in Pennsylvania	Appalachian orogeny began Antler orogeny	Ferns abundant Major coal–forming forests First reptiles
Permian *290–248 million years ago* Named for Russian province of Perm	Pangea formed	First warm–blooded reptiles Greatest mass extinction

	Time Period	Tectonic Events	Biological Events
MESOZOIC ERA *248 to 65 million years ago*	**Triassic Period** *248–206 million years ago* Named for three layers in certain European rocks	Pangea completed Major part of Pangea was arid	First flying vertebrates First dinosaurs First mammals Cephalopods abundant
	Jurassic Period *206–144 million hears ago* Named for the Jura Mountains	Atlantic began to open Pangea separated into Gondwana and Laurasia	First birds Cycads abundant
	Cretaceous Period *144–65 million years ago* Named after Latin word for "chalk"	Major volcanism Sevier orogeny Laurentia separated from Eurasia Sierra Nevada batholith	First flowering plants First social insects Mass extinction of dinosaurs

	Time Period	Tectonic Events	Biological Events
CENOZOIC ERA • *65 million years ago to present* — **TERTIARY PERIOD** • *65 to 1.8 million years ago*	**Paleocene Epoch** *65 to 54.8 million years ago*	Laramide orogeny Western Laurentia uplifted	Mammals and birds diversified First horse ancestors
	Eocene Epoch *54.8 to 33.7 million years ago*	Rockies uplifted Global cooling began	First mammals (whales) in sea First primates First cats and dogs
	Oligocene Epoch *33.7 to 23.8 million years ago*	North Atlantic opened Ice cap formed in Anatarctica	First apes Grasslands widespread
	Miocene Epoch *23.8 to 5.3 million years ago*	Columbia flood basalts	First human ancestors First mastodons
	Pliocene Epoch *5.3 to 1.8 million years ago*	Northern Hemisphere glaciation began Cascade Volcanoes	Large mammals abundant
QUATERNARY PERIOD *1.8 million to today*	**Pleistocene Epoch** *1.8 million years ago to today*	Great glaciation of Northern Hemisphere	First modern humans Extinction of large mammals Humans entered North America
	Holocene *10,000 years ago to today*	Rifting continued in East Africa Human–caused global warming	Human-caused extinctions

GLOSSARY

absolute time dating of rocks and geologic events according to age in years. This is in contrast to relative time, which considers only the order of events.

accretion the addition of terrane to a larger tectonic plate; typically occurs as a result of subduction.

algae (singular is **alga**) simple, often one-celled plants that live in water, such as pond scum or seaweed, with natural green color often hidden by brown or red tint. These plants lack true roots, stems, or leaves.

andesite dark-colored, igneous rock that produces smaller, cone-shaped volcanoes called stratovolcanoes. This fine-grained rock generally occurs in lava flows.

anticline upward-curving (convex) fold that resembles an arch. The central part of this rock structure contains the oldest section of rock.

archaea living cells that are able to survive extremely hot or poisonous conditions. Sometimes called "extremophiles," they date to 3.8 billion years ago.

asthenosphere the part of Earth's mantle that lies beneath the lithosphere. This zone of soft, easily changed, or deformed, rock is believed to be less rigid, hotter, and more fluid than rock above or below.

bacteria (singular is **bacterium**) tiny, one-celled organisms that can be seen only with a microscope

basalt dark, dense, volcanic, extrusive, igneous rock that generally occurs in lava flows. Basalt makes up most of the ocean floor.

bedrock the bottom or lowest layer of continental rock; solid rock that lies beneath soil and other loose surface materials

brachiopod a shelled, clamlike marine animal without a backbone but with tentacles

Canadian Shield largest area of exposed Precambrian rock on Earth. This ancient rock of the North American craton covers more than 1.8 million square miles (4.8 million sq km) from the Great Lakes to the Canadian Arctic to Greenland.

chert very fine-grained sedimentary rock made of quartz. Black chert is known as flint.

cinder cone a fairly small volcano consisting of loose debris blasted out of a larger volcano

composite volcano another name for **stratovolcano**

continental drift early name for **plate tectonics**

continental shelf the part of a continent that is submerged in a shallow sea, thus forming an underwater shelf, before dropping to the seafloor.. Marine life first developed on continental shelves of the Paleozoic supercontinents.

convection currents circular heat currents in Earth's mantle that contribute to the movement of tectonic plates. Heat rises through magma toward the lithosphere, cools, and descends again.

convergent moving toward each other. Convergent boundaries between tectonic plates are active, perhaps building mountains.

core the interior part of Earth beginning at about 1,800 miles (2,900 km) below Earth's surface. Composed mostly of iron alloys, it is divided into two parts: the outer core, which is mostly liquid, and the inner core, which is solid.

craton usually stable, unchanging mass of rock in Earth's crust that forms the basic rock of a continent

crust outermost, rocky layer of Earth. This low-density layer is about 22 miles (35 km) thick under continents and 6 mi (10 km) thick under oceans.

cyanobacteria bacteria that are capable of producing their own food by photosynthesis

deformation the changes in shape, dimension, or volume of rocks that result from folding, faulting, and other processes. Layers of sedimentary rock react to pressure by forcing layers to bend or break.

density state of being dense or compact; weight per unit volume of a substance, usually expressed in grams per cubic centimeter

divergent moving away from each other. Divergent boundaries between tectonic plates are inactive and sediment usually accumulates.

electron a negatively charged particle in an atom that orbits around the nucleus

eon largest division of geologic time, comprising two or more eras. The eons are, from oldest to youngest, the Hadean, Archean, Proterozoic, and Phanerozoic Eons.

epicenter the place on the surface of the earth above the point where an earthquake occurs

extrusive of igneous rock, cooled and solidified quickly at or near the earth's surface; extrusive rock is often called volcanic rock

fault a fracture, or break, in rock along which each side has moved relative to the other. Sudden movements on faults are earthquakes.

fault scarp a steep slope or cliff caused by faulting of the earth's crust.

fjord a narrow passageway from the sea between cliffs or tall hills, often reaching deeply inland, generally carved by glaciers

flood basalt rock produced by massive oozing of lava from large cracks in the earth's crust

fold a noticeable curve in the layering of sedimentary or metamorphic rock. Large-scale folding of rock can create mountains.

fossil evidence or trace of animal or plant life of a past geological age. These typically mineralized remains have been preserved in rocks of the earth's crust. Traces include bones and footprints of extinct land animals, such as dinosaurs.

fungi (singular is **fungus**) a kingdom of organisms that live as parasites on other organisms; formerly regarded as plants that did not carry on photosynthesis

genetic having to do with or produced by genes, the hereditary material of living things

geologic time scale a calendar that establishes distinct time periods in the history of the earth. The time is shown in millions of years. The geologic time scale used in this book is on pages 72 and 73.

geysers hot springs that emit jets of water and steam into the air, like fountains, in an intermittent, or stop-and-start, pattern

glacier a mass of dense ice on land that moves slowly, by coming down from high mountains or spreading out across land from a central point

gneiss a coarse-grained, metamorphic rock, made up of bands that differ in color and composition

granite coarse-grained, intrusive rock. Granite is composed of sodium and potassium feldspar primarily, but it is also rich in quartz. Light in color, it is a common rock in North America.

half-life amount of time needed for one-half the atoms of a radioactive element to turn to another element

heat plume column of hot material in the earth's mantle that rises toward the lithosphere; also called mantle plume

hot spot a place at the bottom of the lithosphere where a heat plume causes rock to melt, especially a spot away from a plate boundary

igneous rock rock formed directly by molten rock cooling and solidifying. *Igneous* means "fiery."

intrusive of volcanic, igneous rock, formed within the earth's crust. Intrusive rocks cooled and crystallized before eventually being lifted to the planet's surface.

ion an atom that is missing an electron, or has an extra one. This electrically charged atom has a negative or a positive charge.

island arc a curved chain of volcanic islands formed along a trench, or subduction zone, such as Alaska's Aleutian Islands

Laurentia a large continent formed during the Paleozoic Era from which the modern continent of North America developed. It was composed mostly of North America and Greenland.

lava fluid, molten rock, or magma, that emerges from a volcano or volcanic vent to the earth's surface. When lava is cooled and solidified, it forms an igneous rock such as basalt.

limestone a type of sedimentary rock made up of more than 50% calcium carbonate ($CaCO_3$), primarily as the mineral calcite.

lithosphere the hard outer layer of Earth containing the outer part of Earth's mantle and crust. It consists of tectonic plates that float on the asthenosphere.

magma molten rock that exists beneath the earth's crust. Magma that flows to the surface is called lava.

magnetic field the measurable force that is present in a magnet or electrical current. The source of the earth's magnetic field is its core, which is rich in iron.

mantle thick part of Earth's interior that lies between the crust and the outer core. Along with the crust, the upper mantle forms the plates of plate tectonics.

metamorphic rock any rock that was created by a chemical or structural change to rock that already existed, from variations in temperature, pressure, and other geological conditions.

meteorite mass of matter that has reached Earth from outer space

microcontinent any of the large bodies of Earth's crust, formed between 3 and 2.5 billion years ago

molten liquefied by heat

neutron a particle without an electric charge, located in the nucleus of an atom

nucleus 1) the positively charged center of an atom, made up of protons and neutrons; 2) the central part of a living cell, encased in a membrane and containing genetic information

ocean ridge another name for **spreading ridge**

outcrop bedrock that has been exposed above the surface of the ground, not covered by soil

paleontologist scientist who studies the fossil remains of past geological periods

Pangea (also written **Pangaea**) the supercontinent made up of most landmasses and covering about 25 percent of Earth's surface. Formed by the end of the Paleozoic Era, it lasted more than 100 million years.

photosynthesis process by which green plants form food (carbohydrates) from carbon dioxide and water through the action of sunlight on chlorophyll; oxygen is a byproduct

plate tectonics theory that Earth's crust and part of the mantle are broken into about a dozen large and several smaller plates within the lithosphere; they move against and interact with one another

platform the part of the continent's craton located under other rock; with the shield, forms the craton

proton a positively charged particle in the nucleus of an atom

protist a major group of microscopic living things, including protozoa and simple algae, that have their genetic information enclosed in a nucleus in the cell

province a generally large area of crust in which the rock has undergone about the same geologic history

quartzite a metamorphic rock composed of the mineral quartz and deriving from quartz sandstone but without the grains cemented together

radioactive decay breakdown of the nucleus of an element. The number of protons in the nucleus gradually changes, creating an atom of a new element.

reef a large mound or ridge within a body of water, made from the skeletons of such organisms as corals and sponges, cemented together

relative dating process of determining the age of an event that involves placing them in the correct chronological sequence. The number of years ago that the event occurred is not considered.

relative time method of dating rocks that gives chronological sequence rather than specific ages. It is useful in determining the order of sedimentary rocks.

rhyolite dark, fine-grained, extrusive, igneous rock that generally occurs in lava flows rich in silica

sandstone common sedimentary rock made up of sand, including quartz, that is cemented together by silica, clay, calcium carbonate, or iron oxide

seafloor spreading the process that occurs as new crust is formed under the ocean and two tectonic plates are pushed apart by great quantities of new volcanic rock. This rock is formed as magma oozing out from between the tectonic plates. Continents riding on these plates are also pushed apart.

sediment loose, uncemented pieces of rock or minerals are carried and deposited by water, air, or ice. Sediment may include eroded sand, dirt particles, debris from living things, and solid materials that form as a result of chemical processes.

sedimentary rock rock composed of sediment, such as sandstone and limestone. Sedimentary rocks typically form beds, or layers.

seismic caused by or pertaining to an earthquake or vibration of the earth

seismic wave a wave of energy that travels through the earth, especially ones given off by an earthquake; can be recorded by an instrument called a seismomenter

shale finely layered sedimentary rock derived from mud formed by the hardening of clay, mud, or silt. When it is not layered, it is known as mudstone. About 70% of Earth's sedimentary rock is shale.

shield volcano a volcano that forms a broad and fairly flat structure, usually because basalt lava flows easily

silica silicon dioxide (SiO_2) compounds that often take a crystalline form. Silica especially occurs as quartz, sand, flint, and agate. Almost 60% of Earth's crust is composed of silica.

stratovolcano fairly small, cone-shaped volcano produced by volcanic rock called andesite and built up both by lava flows and volcanic rock fragments; also called composite volcano

stromatolite layered, limestone fossil structure, probably built by algae and cyanobacteria and having a rounded or columnlike form

subduction the movement of one tectonic plate underneath another and down into the asthenosphere; occurs at trenches, or subduction zones

supercontinent any of probably several giant landmasses formed during Precambrian and Paleozoic times and made up of several present-day continents

syncline a fold of rock layers that is convex or sloped downward. This is the opposite of an anticline, which is convex or sloped upwards.

tectonic plate large section of Earth's lithosphere that floats on the asthenosphere and moves independently, sometimes rubbing against other plates

terrane a fragment of crust that is bounded on all sides by faults and which has a geologic history that differs from neighboring blocks. It may be made from island arcs or a piece of a tectonic plate.

transform fault a vertical fracture in which rock on one side slides past the other. Transform faults connect ocean ridges because of the curve of Earth's surface.

trilobite small crablike shelled animal (or a close relative) present at the beginning of the Paleozoic Era and now extinct

tsunami a large wave that travels along the surface of the ocean set off by an earthquake; sometimes called a tidal wave, but tsunamis have nothing to do with tides

tundra the region toward the poles where only low-growing plants can survive in soil that thaws in summer but remains frozen underneath

viscous resistant to flow

xenolith rock fragment that is foreign to the igneous rock in which it is found; "foreign rock" in Greek

FURTHER INFORMATION

ONLINE WEB SITES

Museum of Paleontology
University of California at Berkeley
1101 Valley Life Sciences Building
Berkeley, CA 94720
www.ucmp.berkeley.edu/exhibit/exhibits.html
takes you through major exhibits in geology,
evolution, and the classification of living things
Also produced by UCMP is:
www.paleoportal.org
provides a link to many sites for anyone
interested in paleontology

United States Geological Survey
USGS National Center
12201 Sunrise Valley Drive
Reston, VA 20192
www.usgs.gov/education
The Learning Web introduces numerous topics and
projects related to earth science
Find out what's happening at Mount St. Helens
volcano: http://volcanoes.usgs.gov
or where the earthquakes are:
http://earthquake.usgs.gov

The British Broadcasting Corporation has major coverage of prehistoric life:
http://www.bbc.co.uk

MUSEUMS

Be sure to look for museum web sites. Also, be sure to check university and public
museums in your area; they often have good geology exhibits.

UNITED STATES
American Museum of Natural History
Central Park West at 79th St.
New York, NY 10024
www.amnh.org

Colorado School of Mines Geology Museum
13th and Maple St.
Golden, CO 80401

The Field Museum
1400 S. Lake Shore Drive
Chicago, IL 60605
www.fieldmuseum.org
Look for the online exhibit about Sue, the best
preserved *Tyrannosaurus rex*

University of Michigan Museum of Paleontology
1109 Geddes Ave.,
Ann Arbor, MI 48109
www.paleontology.lsa.umich.edu

Smithsonian National Museum of Natural History
10th St. and Constitution Ave.
Washington, D.C. 20560
www.mnh.si.edu

CANADA
Geological Survey of Canada
Earth Sciences Sector
601 Booth St.
Ottawa, Ontario K1A 0E8, Canada
http://ess.nrcan.gc.ca

Canadian Museum of Nature
240 McLeod St.
Ottawa, Ontario K1P 6P4, Canada
www.nature.ca

Provincial Museum of Alberta
12845 102nd Ave.
Edmonton, Alberta T5N 0M6, Canada
www.prma.edmonton.ab.ca

Manitoba Museum of Man and Nature
190 Rupert Avenue
Winnipeg, Manitoba R3B 0N2, Canada
www.manitobamuseum.mb.ca

Pacific Museum of the Earth
6339 Stores Road
Vancouver, British Columbia V6T 1Z4, Canada
www.eos.ubc.ca

DVDs

Amazing Earth, Artisan Entertainment, 2001

Forces of Nature—Book and DVD, National Geographic, 2004

Living Rock: An Introduction to Earth's Geology, WEA Corp, 2002
Also includes 400 USGS "Fact Sheets" in Adobe Acrobat format, obtainable on computer sytems with a
   DVD-ROM Drive)

Physical Geography: Geologic Time, TMW/Media Group, 2004

Volcano: Nature's Inferno!, National Geographic, 1997

BOOKS

Anderson, Peter. *A Grand Canyon Journey: Tracing Time in Stone.* A First Book. Danbury, CT:
   Franklin Watts, 1997.

Ball, Jacqueline. *Earth's History.* Discovery Channel School Science series. Milwaukee, WI: Gareth
   Stevens Publishing, 2004.

Bonner, Hannah. *When Bugs Were Big : Prehistoric Life in a World Before Dinosaurs.* Washington, DC:
   National Geographic, 2004.

Castelfranchi, Yuri, and Nico Petrilli. *History of the Earth: Geology, Ecology, and Biology.* Hauppage,
   NY: Barrons, 2003.

Colson, Mary. *Earth Erupts.* Turbulent Earth series. Chicago: Raintree, 2005.

Colson, Mary. *Shaky Ground.* Turbulent Earth series. Chicago: Raintree, 2005.

Day, Trevor. *DK Guide to Savage Earth: An Earth Shattering Journey of Discovery.* New York: Dorling
   Kindersley, 2001.

Farndon, John. *How the Earth Works.* Pleasantville, NY: Reader's Digest, 1992.

Hooper, Meredith. *The Pebble in My Pocket: A History of Our Earth.* New York: Viking Books, 1996.

Lambert, David. *The Kingfisher Young People's Book of the Universe.* Boston: Kingfisher, 2001.

Maslin, Mark. *Earthquakes.* Restless Planet series. Chicago: Raintree, 2000.

Maynard, Christopher. *My Book of the Prehistoric World.* Boston: Kingfisher, 2001.

Oxlade, Chris. *The Earth and Beyond.* Chicago: Heinemann Library, 1999.

NOTE: All Internet addresses (URLs) listed in this book were valid at the time it went to press.
However, due to the dynamic nature of the Internet, some addresses may have changed, or sites
may have ceased to exist since publication. While the authors and publisher regret any inconvenience
this may cause readers, no responsibility for any such changes can be accepted by either the authors
or publisher.